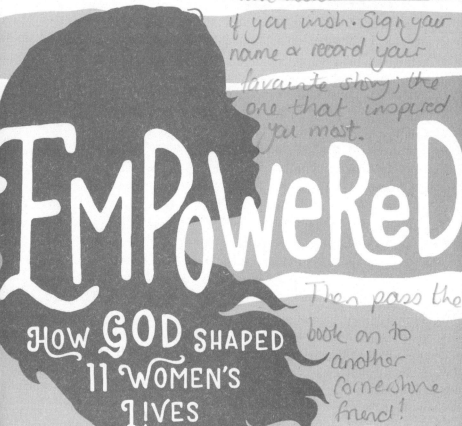

If you wish. Sign your name & record your favourite story; the one that inspired you most.

Then pass the book on to another Cornerstone friend!

Jamie p.

EMPOWERED

HOW GOD SHAPED 11 WOMEN'S LIVES

(AND CAN SHAPE YOURS TOO)

CATHERINE PARKS

ILLUSTRATIONS BY BREEZY BROOKSHIRE

B&H
PUBLISHING GROUP
Nashville, Tennessee

978-1-5359-3455-8

Published by B&H Publishers Group
Nashville, Tennessee

Dewey Decimal Classification: 248.83
Subject Heading: GOD / CHRISTIAN LIFE / GIRLS

1 2 3 4 5 6 7 • 22 21 20 19

For Sophie, our Wisdom Child.
Being your mother brings me immeasurable
joy. Our Father, who empowered each of these
women, is working in you, and I'm so thankful
I get to be a witness to His work.

James 3:17

ACKNOWLEDGMENTS

Each woman in this book was only able to do what she did because she was empowered by God and encouraged and helped by others. I'm so thankful that God gave me the opportunity to write this and sent the helpers I needed along the way.

The team at B&H understood the vision and worked with me to refine and produce it. Thanks to Devin Maddox, Holly Spangle, Michelle Burke, Dave Schroeder, and many others. Your excitement and encouragement have been sweet gifts during the process.

The extremely talented Breezy Brookshire created the beautiful images that surpassed what I had imagined. Thank you for using your gifts on this project! I'm so grateful.

Thanks to those who helped me land on these eleven women, particularly Kristie Anyabwile, who recommended Phillis and Charlotte, both incredible women.

I'm indebted to the many biographers whose countless hours of research and writing allowed me to produce this book.

Ava Newell and my daughter, Sophie, were willing early readers, and their feedback was so helpful.

Thanks to my Saturday morning girls, who prayed and cheered me on.

I'm thankful for the many women in my life who embody so many of the qualities of these women, especially Laura, Liesl, Jen, Amber, Trillia, and the ladies of the I.D.K. Society.

My family has been so supportive. Thank you, Mom, Dad, Roger, and Carol for your interest and prayers.

Sophie and Micah, I hope learning about these women encourages you about what God can do. You are recipients of a great heritage of faithful women who love Jesus. Your Father is shaping your lives and working in you, and I love watching it happen!

Erik, you have empowered me to do what I love. Thanks for giving your time and energy to help me get this done. Many of the women in this book were married to men who greatly cheered and supported their wives' ministries and vocations. Reading about them made me even more grateful for you. I love you.

CONTENTS

READ THIS FIRST

I'm so excited you picked up this book! I've spent months learning about the women in these chapters—so long, in fact, that I've started referring to them as if they were my personal friends. My kids often hear me saying things like, "Listen to what Annie wrote to a friend," and "Can you believe what Phillis got to see in England?" And now it's a joy to introduce you to my new friends. You may have heard of some of them, while others are probably new names and faces.

We remember these women because of events in their lives that made them famous or noteworthy. But I want you to meet them *before* those events happened. When Joni Eareckson Tada was seventeen, she wasn't trying to become an internationally known speaker and artist. Before the Nazis took over Holland, Corrie and Betsie ten Boom hadn't planned to save hundreds of people's lives. When Fanny Crosby was a little girl, she wasn't thinking about writing thousands of hymns.

Not one woman in this book planned to become famous or change the world. Their lives took them in many different directions—as missionaries, artists, prisoners, teachers, poets, songwriters, martyrs, speakers, and mothers. They lived in different places, spoke different languages, wore different clothes, and had different ethnic backgrounds.

But all of them had one thing in common— they truly knew God.

If you went to a store today and read the messages on T-shirts for girls and teens, or walked through a bookstore and looked at books for girls, you'd probably see a lot of the same thing: messages saying your purpose is to *do* something, dream big, make a difference. You might even be reading this book because it seems like a good way to learn how to accomplish big things with your life. After all, each of the women in this book is famous for doing something important, so maybe you can learn something from their lives that will help you.

In fact, you *can*. But it's not what a lot of people might expect.

The Bible doesn't tell us our purpose in life is to do big things or change the world. Instead, it says we're created in the image of God—we're made to show the world the glory of God!

Just like the women in this book, we do this first and foremost by knowing God.

When the women in the following pages were tested by suffering and difficulties, they had the tools they needed to stand up under pressure: they had hidden God's Word in their hearts, and they knew God answers His children's prayers. They didn't just know *about* God, they knew Him personally.

While many people call these women heroines of faith, they were actually a lot like you and me.

One of the most encouraging things I discovered when reading about these women was not how amazing they were, but how *normal* they were. They had fights with friends, acted selfishly, wanted to be liked, were afraid, didn't like certain subjects in school, etc. They were normal girls and women, empowered in supernatural ways.

And here's great news: you can have the same supernatural power! My hope and prayer is that as you read about each of these women, you will see who the true hero is: God.

God created you in order to have a relationship with you. But because you (and I and everyone who ever lived) broke God's Law—His plan for how we should live—we can't be in that relationship with Him. So He made a plan to fix the things we all messed up. He sent His Son, Jesus, to earth to become a man and live a perfect life, never sinning. Then, because the punishment for our sin is death, Jesus took all our sin upon Himself and died in our place. But to show that He has victory over death, God raised Jesus back up from the grave, and He went back to heaven, where He waits to one day come back and unite with the Father all those who have trusted in Him as the Way to God. But Jesus didn't just leave us without help—when He went back to heaven, the Father sent us the Holy Spirit. This means that when we trust Jesus, we have the Holy Spirit living in our hearts, helping us daily to understand the Bible and to follow Jesus.

The Spirit of God living inside you?! It doesn't get more supernatural than that.

This is why the book is called *Empowered*—because God daily gives us the power we need to reflect His glory, to love Him, and to love others, just as He did for all the women in this book. This love takes many forms, reflected in the different qualities we see in each chapter. Loving God and others means standing up for justice, being selfless, using our gifts, and many other things. But the power to do those things comes from God, not from our own strength. We won't ever do these things perfectly, but the good news is that God forgives and uses imperfect people!

Be encouraged to recognize the unique way in which He's made you. You are exactly who you're supposed to be—not the next Elisabeth Elliot or the next Pandita Ramabai or the next Charlotte Grimké. God created *you* with your unique abilities and desires. Your job isn't to be like these women; it is to bring yourself to the table and ask God how He wants to use you—not necessarily to change the world in a grand way, but to do the little things that add up to a faithful life. Real change happens in the world when we're faithful to do what He gives us to do in His power.

I wrote this book because I wanted my daughter, Sophie, and my nieces, Liya and Madelyn, to know about these women. But my greater purpose was for Sophie and *you* to know that God has a plan for your life right where you are and that He will empower you to accomplish your purpose each and every day.

Paul's words to some of his friends are my words to you as well:

> I am sure of this, that he who started a good work in you will carry it on to completion until the day of Christ Jesus.—Philippians 1:6

God is faithful—He will help you and work in and through you.

Now let's find out how He did that in these eleven women's lives!

"I knew it would be impossible for me to keep my faith in my own power. God would have to work through me if I was to stand firm."

ESTHER AHN KIM
TRUE STRENGTH

Ahn Ei Sook (later known by her married name, Esther Ahn Kim) was born in 1908. She grew up in a time when her home country, Korea, was occupied and ruled by Japan. The Japanese military forced Koreans to adopt Japanese customs, including their Shinto religion, which involved worshiping nature spirits, ancestors, and the emperor. Ei Sook's family was divided, with her mother following Christ and her father's family practicing idol worship.

Strong-willed as a child, Ei (pronounced "Ay") Sook (rhymes with "took") had her hair cut short like a boy's because she couldn't stand having it brushed. She hated seeing her grandmother worship idols, wondering how someone so religious could still be so miserable. On one festival day, she crept into the room where they kept the food that was to be sacrificed to the idols. She yelled at the idols, saying, "Why do you eat the best foods and then make my grandmother unhappy?

Die eating the food mixed with my spittle!" And she proceeded to spit on her finger and rub her saliva on all of the foods. But this wasn't enough. She then put horse dung on the end of a walking stick and touched it to each idol basket, saying, "You demons! Why can't you make happiness and peace? Why do you make Grandmother unpleasant and upset while she worships you? Eat horse droppings and die!"

One night before she fell asleep, her mother told her, "As you can see, idols have no power at all. The Lord Jesus is the only One who can give us true power and happiness and peace." Because God worked through her mother's faith, Ei Sook also trusted Him and followed Jesus.

Ei Sook's mother wanted her daughter to attend a mission school, but her father insisted she receive a Japanese education, first at a public school in Korea and then at a college in Japan. She studied in Japan long enough to become fluent in the language and to grow to love the people, but she couldn't have imagined how God would use this knowledge and love later on.

She came home to Korea and taught music at a Christian school. One day, the Japanese leaders took everyone from the school and the surrounding community to a shrine (a "holy" place) where they were forced to worship a false Japanese god. If they refused, the school would be closed and they would be tortured. Shrines were placed in every school, government office, home, and Christian church. Police would come to church services to make sure that every person bowed to the Shinto god before the service began.

As Ei Sook walked to the shrine, she remembered how Shadrach, Meshach, and Abednego had refused to bow to the statue of the Babylonian King Nebuchadnezzar in the Bible. They knew God had the power to deliver them, but they said even if He didn't save them, they still wouldn't bow. They would honor God even to death. Ei Sook decided she would do the same. "Today on the mountain, before the large crowd," she silently

3

prayed, "I will proclaim that there is no other God beside You. This is what I will do for Your holy name."

The order came for everyone to bow to the sun goddess, and the massive crowd all bowed—all except Ei Sook. As she thought about the torture to come as punishment, she remembered the words of a hymn that encouraged her that Jesus was on her side:

> Did we in our own strength confide,
> Our striving would be losing;
> Were not the right Man on our side,
> The Man of God's own choosing:
> Dost ask who that may be?
> Christ Jesus, it is He; Lord Sabaoth His
>   Name,
> From age to age the same,
> And He must win the battle.
> —Martin Luther

When she returned to the school, four detectives were waiting for her. God gave her peace as they arrested her and took her to the district chief. But in the middle of his angry speech to her, the phone rang and he had to rush out of the office. Ei Sook quickly got up and ran out of the building and back to her home. She knew she could not stay, however. She disguised herself as a country woman and went into hiding.

As she rode on a train through the black night, she looked out at the stars shining brightly in the dark sky. *True faith should be like those stars,* she thought, *shining even brighter as the world becomes darker.* She later wrote how she looked out, wishing "to shine in the black night sky of my beloved country like a changeless star."

In hiding, Ei Sook prepared for the day when she would be captured and put in prison. She knew she wouldn't have a Bible there, so she memorized more than one hundred Bible chapters and many hymns. She fasted from food for days at a time and slept in the cold, trying to prepare her body for the harsh conditions of prison.

After a time of hiding in the country, the Lord led her to go to the city of Pyongyang. She didn't know what to expect there, but as she arrived, she saw a train loaded with young Japanese soldiers, headed for the battlefields in China. She had a strong sense that someone must go to the Japanese leaders and tell them they were sending these young men to death and hell. But who?

While in Pyongyang, Ei Sook met with many other Christians. They came and went in secret, some having been recently released from prison. All of them knew prison might be in their future. They heard descriptions of the torture fellow believers had faced, and Ei Sook cried at the thought of what she might experience.

One day a man named Elder Park came to her house and said God had told him to go to Pyongyang to see her. He said, "Everyone is so afraid that no one warns Japan. I have already been chosen by His holy voice. You have been chosen, too, haven't you?"

Ei Sook was afraid to speak.

"You speak Japanese, don't you?" Elder Park asked.

"Yes," she answered.

"That is what we need: your good Japanese," Elder Park said. "But I have come to understand that you are a beautiful believer. What good can your excellent language do without faith? God has led me here so that He can use you."

Yet Ei Sook found excuses for why she shouldn't go. She wrote, "Elder Park was a brave soldier of Christ who could fearlessly warn the Japanese government, but I was merely a woman, and besides, I was afraid."

She knew going to Japan could mean torture or even death. She wanted God to give her a sign that she should go. But her mother told her it was wrong to ask God for what the Bible doesn't say. "The Bible is our guide," she said. So Ei Sook fasted, prayed, and read her Bible for three days. She knew God was calling her to go to Japan, and she knew that being beaten, starved, or killed would be better than disobeying Him. She would go with Elder Park to Japan.

Now it was clear: Ei Sook's Japanese education and her God-given love for Japan had a purpose. Yet the path was dangerous. Elder Park couldn't get a passport to travel to Japan because he had previously been a prisoner. But while this worried Ei Sook, Elder Park had no fear. He knew God would make a way for them to do what He had called them to do. And that's just what happened—God miraculously caused the police to pass right over Elder Park on the train, not even seeing him. The same thing happened when they boarded a ship. God was making their path straight.

The Japanese people, and even many of the country's leaders, didn't know how their countrymen were treating Koreans. Ei Sook and Elder Park were able to meet with some of the leaders and warn them about God's judgment. They told them they believed Japan would suffer God's judgment by fire falling from the sky if they did not turn from their sin against Him and His people.

One day Elder Park and Ei Sook were able to go to the Imperial Diet—the meeting of the highest officials in Japan. The rules for attending were very strict in order to avoid disturbing the meeting. But in the middle of the assembly, Elder Park dropped a sign down from the balcony. On it, he had written a message calling the Japanese government to repent and withdraw from Korea and to examine which was the true religion— Shintoism or Christianity. Immediately, Elder Park and Ei Sook were arrested.

For six years, from 1939 to 1945, Ei Sook lived in a Japanese prison in Korea. She was given the number fifty-seven to replace her name, and she listened as the female jailers yelled at the prisoners. Ei Sook prayed, "The rest of the world has completely disappeared from me. I am a weakling. Unless I live each day holding Your hand, I'll become too frightened. Lord, hold my hand firmly so I won't part from You. Jesus, I love You."

Over the next six years, Ei Sook experienced joy and sorrow in abundance. She and her fellow prisoners were constantly hungry and frequently extremely cold. Many of the jailers and guards were harsh and hateful. But the Lord also brought jailers who loved Ei Sook and became Christians. One such woman, Jue, came because she wanted to learn from pastors and she knew most of them were in prison. So she got a job at the prison so she could be taught about Jesus.

Many of her fellow prisoners trusted Christ because of Ei Sook's love for them and the witness of her faith. She loved the unlovable—the angry, dirty, proud, and mentally ill. Repeatedly, she cried out to God for strength, knowing how weak she was. One fellow prisoner was known for being dangerous. She would bite and attack guards, and she had to have her hands tied behind her back at all times. Ei Sook asked that this woman be brought into her cell. Everyone thought she was crazy, but she insisted. This woman's clothes were covered in filth, and she fought Ei Sook to the point that they were wrestling on the ground.

Eventually, the prisoner fell asleep as Ei Sook held her feet to warm them. She slept for three days straight. When she awoke, she ate her food and then still glared angrily at Ei Sook. Writing later, Ei Sook said:

> Jesus Himself was participating in this battle, I realized. Surely my gratitude was beyond words. By nature, I would have tried to ignore the girl with all my might, but in reality exactly the opposite was happening. Here I was, holding a woman who was unspeakably dirty. Only Jesus' mercy could cause me to do it.
>
> Jesus knew I was selfish, weak, deceitful, and sinful. But He treated me as valuable and important. How could I avoid her simply because she was so dirty in my eyes? To Him, we were the same.

Ei Sook told this woman that she loved her, and as she did, a miracle happened in her heart—she really did love and even *like* this woman! Ei Sook gave up her meals to her, combed her tangled hair, told her she was pretty. The jailers noticed that this woman—prisoner number ninety-two—had changed. But she changed still more as Ei Sook shared the good news about Jesus with her. She gave her life to Christ, believing that everyone is a sinner and Jesus alone could save her. Prisoner Ninety-Two was executed for her crimes, but she walked willingly to her death, knowing she would soon be with her Savior.

There is much more to Ei Sook's story in prison, many more people affected by the Holy Spirit's work through her. But on August 15, 1945, Japan surrendered, and the prisoners were soon released. Sadly, this was not the end of Korea's suffering, as the country was divided into two regions, and many Christians continue to face persecution in the North. When she was released, Ei Sook learned that fire had indeed rained down on Japan from bombs. Entire cities were on fire. She grieved for the many Japanese who had died without hearing the gospel, and she wondered what had become of the leaders who had ignored and laughed at her warnings.

Today, God continues to use Ei Sook's life and testimony for His glory. She wrote her story in a book that quickly became the all-time religious best seller in Korea and then became a best seller in Japan as well. But she didn't want people to think she was amazing—her story is about a strong God working through a weak woman:

> It was an unbelievable privilege for a person like me, sinful, selfish, conceited, and with many faults, to receive an order from God, who was the Lord of the heavens and earth. I was overwhelmed. In spite of my weakness and sinfulness, the Lord had given me the grace to walk and work with Him.

SOURCE

Esther Ahn Kim, *If I Perish* (Chicago: Moody Publishers, 2001).

EMPOWERED WITH STRENGTH

We have a lot of ideas about what strength is. It might be physical—the ability to lift something heavy. Or mental strength—staying tough and not giving up when you want to quit something. Sometimes we think spiritual strength means not sinning and always loving others.

The apostle Paul wrote about spiritual strength in 2 Corinthians 12:9–10. He had begged God to give him power and deliverance from something difficult in his life, but God responded differently. Paul writes:

> But he said to me, "My grace is sufficient for you, for my power is perfected in weakness."
>
> Therefore, I will most gladly boast all the more about my weaknesses, so that Christ's power may reside in me. So I take pleasure in weaknesses, insults, hardships, persecutions, and in

difficulties, for the sake of Christ. For
when I am weak, then I am strong.

Ei Sook lived this out, seeing her own weakness over and over again. She knew she needed
a strength outside of herself—the power of Jesus
Christ.

You will probably never face imprisonment for
your faith. You may not be called to give a warn-
ing to national leaders. But you will see your own
weakness—in school, in relationships with friends
and family, in your struggle with sin. Know that
this is a good thing! When we are weak, He is
strong in us!

The same power working in Ei Sook in prison
is at work in you *right now.* You don't have to do
anything amazing to have that power—just ask
Him to work His strength in you and praise Him
when He does!

QUESTIONS

1. Read Philippians 2:13–16. What element of nature does Paul compare Christians to? What are we supposed to do? How do we do it?

2. How is this similar to Ei Sook's thoughts as she gazed out at the night sky on the train? How did she follow the teaching of Philippians 2:13–16?

3. Where has God placed you that is dark and needs light?

4. Read John 8:12. Where does our light come from?

5. Are you ever discouraged by your sin and weakness? Are you afraid to share the good news about Jesus with others? How does Ei Sook's story encourage you?

"I AM THE LIGHT OF THE WORLD. ANYONE WHO FOLLOWS ME WILL NEVER WALK IN THE DARKNESS BUT WILL HAVE THE LIGHT OF LIFE." —JOHN 8:12

"How can we expect righteousness to prevail when there is hardly anyone who will give himself up undividedly to a righteous cause?"

SOPHIE SCHOLL
SEEKING JUSTICE

Sophie Scholl (pronounced "Shole") grew up in a German town circled by forests. She and her brothers and sisters spent their days having adventures, picking berries and mushrooms, and performing theatrical plays with just the trees and bushes as their audience. She loved swimming and being around water. In the spring, often the streets in her town flooded, and it was difficult to walk. Her father bought stilts for his children, which they used to cross over the streets like adventurers.

No childhood adventure could prepare her for the things she would experience as a teenager, however. When she was twelve years old, Sophie's country, Germany, came under the control of a new leader, Adolf Hitler. Many Germans thought things would be much better for them under this new leadership, but Sophie's father disagreed. He asked his children to look around and see that Hitler and his officials were taking away the freedoms that Germans had—freedom to have their own opinions and ideas and beliefs. Germany was quickly becoming a country where people were told what they could and could not think and say.

Soon Sophie and her siblings were required to join clubs that taught them what to think and say. They were kept so busy that they had no time to sit and talk or have their own ideas. Instead of being taught to seek the good of all people, they were instructed that some people were not worth as much as others. They were taught to hate certain groups of people. Sophie saw some of her classmates being excluded from these clubs because they were Jewish. At first few people thought much about this, but over time Jewish people were required to wear a badge and hang signs on their businesses letting everyone know they were Jews.

Because people were not encouraged to think for themselves, they believed their leaders when they told them their Jewish neighbors could not be trusted. Soon, all the Jewish people were moved out of their homes and forced to live in one area of their cities. They were not permitted to walk around at certain times of day. They were guarded by angry men and yelled at by children and adults on the streets. Imagine being taught your whole life that your neighbor was a wicked person and watching others yell at him and his family. You, too, might join in, because you wouldn't know better. This is what it was like for many young children living in Germany at that time.

Eventually, all the Jewish people began to disappear. The German people were told their Jewish neighbors had been moved to work camps, where they could work to make ammunition for the war they were fighting against other countries. This was partly true, but many Germans didn't know that these camps were used to kill millions of Jewish people and other groups of people that Hitler and his officials did not like.

Sophie noticed things were not right. She was tired of being told what to think. The more she learned about Hitler and others in control in Germany, the more she was convinced he had to be stopped. When she was twenty-one, she joined her brother Hans and his friends in a secret organization called The White Rose. They wrote, printed, and handed out papers that challenged what people were told to think. Instead of just believing what Hitler was telling them, The White Rose asked people to wake up and look around at their country. They secretly passed their papers out at colleges in the hope that other students would start to ask questions and talk about how to take their country back from Hitler.

Being part of The White Rose was extremely dangerous. Sophie and Hans knew that if anyone found out they were the ones distributing these papers, they would be arrested and accused of high treason (acting against their country's government). The punishment for treason was death. But Sophie, Hans, and the others working with them believed they had to do something to stand up against the wrong being done to millions of people. They knew the risk and acted anyway.

On Thursday, February 18, 1943, Sophie and Hans went to the University of Munich with a small suitcase full of papers calling others to stand up against Hitler. While the students were in their classes, Sophie and Hans went through the halls placing stacks of papers outside the classroom doors. After walking out with their suitcase, they realized it still had papers in it. They went back into the university, stood at the top of an open courtyard, leaned over the rail, and pushed the papers to float down on students just coming out of their classes. Hans and Sophie walked away, trying to blend in with other students, but a janitor had seen them. He grabbed their arms and yelled, "You are under arrest!"

Soon, Hans and Sophie found themselves being interrogated (questioned) by Robert Mohr, a Gestapo officer. The Gestapo was the name of the Secret Police Hitler had created. Their job was to carry out Hitler's wishes and to punish those who dared to disobey any of their rules. Mohr asked both Sophie and Hans many questions, and Gestapo officers went to their apartments and found evidence that pointed to their involvement in The White Rose. They also arrested one of their friends, Christoph Probst. All three were accused of high treason.

Even after being questioned for hours—all through the night—Sophie was peaceful. The woman she shared a cell with in the Gestapo prison wrote about Sophie: "You slept deeply. How I admired you! All those hours of interrogation had done nothing to your calm, relaxed manner. Your unshakable, deep faith gave you strength to sacrifice yourself for others."

Mohr tried to get Sophie to change her mind or to say perhaps she had been wrong. He told her she and Hans had been wrong about Germany's inability to win the war. He said, "Miss Scholl, if you had considered all this, you wouldn't have allowed yourself to be carried away with activities of that kind, now would you?" But Sophie bravely replied, "You are wrong. I would do everything again, exactly the same way. For it is not I who have the wrong philosophy of life, it is you."

Two days later, Sophie, Hans, and Christoph were taken before a judge who sentenced them to death for their acts of treason. In their final meeting with their parents, they hugged and comforted one another. Sophie's parents offered her a piece of candy, and she gladly accepted it, enjoying this small pleasure amid terrible circumstances. She was concerned about her mother, who would soon lose two of her children. Her mother said to her, "Remember, Sophie: Jesus." Sophie replied, "Yes—but you must remember too." Then she left.

The warden (the man in charge of the prison) later wrote a report about Hans, Sophie, Christoph, and their final moments. "They were so incredibly brave," he wrote. "The entire prison was impressed." The three were given a few moments together; then they were led away, one at a time. Sophie went first. "She went without batting an eyelash," the warden wrote. "None of us could understand how such a thing was possible. The executioner said he had never seen anyone die like that.

"And Hans, before he put his head on the block, cried in a loud voice—you could hear it reverberate throughout the large prison—'Long live freedom!'"

After the war, their interrogator, Robert Mohr, wrote that Sophie and Hans both said "no sacrifice was too great to be offered gladly" if it was possible to help save the lives of German soldiers and people. They tried to take all the blame so that none of their friends would be punished along with them. "Till the very end," Mohr said, "Sophie and Hans Scholl were convinced that their sacrifice was not in vain."

SOURCE

Hermann Vinke, *The Short Life of Sophie Scholl*; translated from the German by Hedwig Pachter (New York: Harper and Row, 1984).

EMPOWERED TO SEEK JUSTICE

Have you ever watched someone being unkind or cruel to another person? Maybe a girl talks meanly about another girl in your class, or a boy pushes around another boy. Maybe you've seen a teacher being unfair to a student. Or perhaps you hear adults or kids talking about people from other countries or backgrounds as if they are less important or not worthy of respect.

Noticing these things is part of growing up. God loves justice, but in our broken world we often see injustice being done to us or to others. It may not be the kind of injustice Sophie saw, but humans are often cruel and unkind to one another. It's hard to know what to do when we see it. Do we say anything? Is it okay to notice it and not do anything? Is it okay to let it go on as long as we aren't joining in?

One of the names for Jesus in the Bible is the "Prince of Peace." We usually think of the word *peace* as meaning "lack of conflict." A peaceful car ride would be one where no one is fighting. We think, *I need to keep the peace, so I shouldn't say anything.*

But in the Bible, *peace* actually means something better—it means "completeness" and "fullness." This isn't just the absence of fighting. If someone is complete and full, they have all they need to grow and enjoy life. It means they are living out their God-given purpose in joy.

As followers of the Prince of Peace, Christians are given the job of spreading this kind of peace to people around us—in our homes, our schools, our neighborhoods, our cities, and around the world. This means when we notice that people aren't complete and full, living in harmony, we should ask why and see what we can do about it. While this usually isn't easy, we serve a God who gives us His Holy Spirit to make us brave and courageous to do what's right.

Most of the time our stand for justice will be in small ways—telling a classmate to stop being unkind or asking a friend to reconsider what they're saying about people who aren't like them.

Sophie's story is not a normal one. Most of us will never be in a situation where we must make such a hard choice to act for justice and face death. But the same God who gave her peace and courage will help you as you take a stand for truth and justice where you are. The same love of Jesus that compelled Sophie to give her life can enable you to stand up for a bullied classmate. He is faithful to help those who spread His peace in their homes, communities, and throughout the world.

QUESTIONS

---

1. Think of a time when you noticed injustice. What did you do? What did you want to do?

2. Read Micah 6:8. What does it say about God's people and justice?

3. God gave Sophie the confidence to tell her interrogator that *he* was the one with the wrong life-philosophy. How can you stand firm in your faith so you're not led astray by other ideas? (For a hint, look at Colossians 2:6–8.)

4. Do you know anyone who has never done anything unjust? Is it possible to do this? What makes it so hard?

5. God is the only One who is truly just all the time. Sin must be punished, but God punished Jesus—who never sinned—in our place. How does knowing this make you feel?

6. Does knowing that you're accepted by God because of Jesus make it easier to seek justice for others? Why?

7. What is one situation where you can spread peace—"completeness" and "fullness"—to those around you?

MANKIND, HE HAS TOLD EACH OF YOU WHAT IS GOOD AND WHAT IT IS THE LORD REQUIRES OF YOU: TO ACT JUSTLY, TO LOVE FAITHFULNESS, AND TO WALK HUMBLY WITH YOUR GOD. —MICAH 6:8

*"Whenever we cannot love in the old, human way . . .
God can give us the perfect way."*

CORRIE TEN BOOM
LOVING THE UNLOVABLE

When I was growing up, my family had a book about a woman named Corrie ten Boom. I never read the book, but I knew from the cover that she had lived in Holland in Europe during World War II and ended up in a Nazi concentration camp. I was always intrigued by her, partly because we share the same birthday. In fact, she also died on her birthday in 1983—the exact day I was born. I felt a connection to her but didn't read about her life until I was much older. Now her book *The Hiding Place* is one of my favorites.

This is a bit of Corrie's story:

Corrie grew up in a three-story home in a small city called Haarlem. Her father was a watchmaker, and his shop was on the ground floor of their home. She had two older sisters, Betsie and Nollie, and a brother, Willem. Their family was not wealthy, but even in times where money was tight, they found a way to share their food and their home with those in need.

The dining room table was "the heart of the home." It was where the children gathered for every meal with their parents and the three aunts who lived with them. With a blanket spread across it, the table became Corrie's tent, pirate's cove, or the location for whatever other adventure she was having in her childhood. As she grew older, it became the homework location or where the children would sit while their mother read aloud to them by the fire.

Corrie loved riding her bike around the city of Haarlem, feeling the wheels bounce on the cobble-stone streets. Even as an adult, this was how she got around town, running errands or visiting friends and family.

Every Monday, Corrie's father, Casper, would take the train to the big city of Amsterdam. It's hard for us to imagine, but in the early 1900s, there were no automatic clocks. You couldn't pull out a cell phone or turn on a computer to see what time it was. It was the watchmaker's job to make watches and to keep them running on time. So every Monday, Casper rode the train to Amsterdam for the purpose of getting the exact time from the Naval Observatory. He didn't have a phone to call someone up and find out the time— he had to go see it for himself and bring the cor- rect time back with him in order to keep all the clocks and watches running for the next week. When Corrie went on these trips with her father, he taught her many things about life and loving others in his gentle, sweet way. She followed in his footsteps and became the first woman licensed as a watchmaker in Holland.

When she was fourteen, Corrie met her older brother Willem's friend Karel. Karel and Willem were in college together, and Corrie fell in love with him the moment she looked into his deep brown eyes. Her sister, Nollie, was two years older than Corrie, and she was used to getting boys' attention. They would often ask her for a lock of her hair (boys used to remember a girl by carry- ing part of her with them), and she would take a few strands from the old gray carpet in the girls' bedroom, tie them with a blue ribbon, and make Corrie deliver it to the boy. Corrie wrote, "The carpet was quite threadbare by now, the school full of broken hearts." Corrie knew she would not get the kind of attention Nollie got, but she wanted so badly to have Karel's attention. Eventually, that's exactly what happened.

When she was twenty-one, they began spending more time together and wrote letters to each other. Corrie was sure it was heading toward marriage. While he had not proposed, he gave every indication he would soon do so.

But one day, he showed up on her family's doorstep with his fiancée. Corrie learned that his parents expected him to marry someone wealthy and from an important family, and he'd agreed. Corrie was heartbroken, unsure if she could forgive and love Karel after he had betrayed her heart. When Karel left, she ran up to her room and sobbed. She heard her father coming up the stairs and was afraid he would try to comfort her by saying, "There'll be someone else soon." But he did not say that.

Instead, he said:

> Corrie, do you know what hurts so very much? It's love. Love is the strongest force in the world, and when it is blocked that means pain. There are two things we can do when this happens. We can kill the love so that it stops hurting. But then of course part of us dies, too. Or, Corrie, we can ask God to open up another route for that love to travel. . . . Whenever we cannot love in the old, human way, Corrie, God can give us the perfect way.

Corrie later said, "I did not know, as I listened to Father's footsteps winding back down the stairs, that he had given me more than the key to this hard moment. I did not know that he had put into my hands the secret that would open far darker rooms than this—places where there was not, on a human level, anything to love at all."

Years after this conversation with her father, Corrie watched Nazi forces invade her home country of Holland. She saw friends and acquaintances disappearing as the Nazis took them away because they were Jewish. Her faith in God and knowledge of His Word compelled her to act. She could not sit by and watch other people made by God being taken away, made to work, and many times killed.

So Corrie decided to do something. She didn't take action in order to be a hero. She had no lofty goal of doing great things. She was simply willing to do what God called her to do in that moment, whether big or small.

Along with their father, Corrie and her sister Betsie arranged for a secret compartment to be built in their home. In this "hiding place," they hid Jews who were in grave danger of being arrested and taken to concentration camps. They would hide these people until they could find a better place for them out in the country or in other homes. Corrie was involved in a secret network of people working together to provide shelter and protection for Jews. Through this network and the hiding place in Corrie's home, they saved nearly eight hundred lives over the course of more than three years.

But this work was extremely dangerous. Corrie, Betsie, and their father, along with other family members, were eventually arrested and sent to prison. Corrie and Betsie were later transferred to Ravensbrück, a concentration camp where they lived under horrible conditions. Forced to work long hours, given little food, enduring sickness, cold, and fleas everywhere, the sisters tried to share the love of Christ with the women around them. For Corrie, though, there were times when loving was almost impossible.

Eventually, Corrie was released from the camp and went on to speak all over the world about the hiding place, her experiences in the concentration camp, and the love of God.

After she finished speaking at an event one night in Munich, Germany, a man came up to Corrie. She recognized him as a Nazi soldier who had stood guard at the shower room door when she and Betsie arrived at Ravensbrück. Seeing him brought back terrifying memories. He came up to her, smiling, and said, "How grateful I am for your message. . . . To think that, as you say, He has washed my sins away!"

Corrie had traveled around the world, telling people to forgive those who hurt them. But in this moment, as this guard stuck out his hand to shake hers, she could not do it. She later said:

> I tried to smile, I struggled to raise my hand. I could not. I felt nothing, not the slightest spark of warmth or charity. And so again I breathed a silent prayer. *Jesus, I cannot forgive him. Give Your forgiveness.*
>
> As I took his hand the most incredible thing happened. From my shoulder along my arm and through my hand, a

current seemed to pass from me to him, while into my heart sprang a love for this stranger that almost overwhelmed me. . . .

When He tells us to love our enemies, He gives, along with the command, the love itself.

SOURCE

Corrie ten Boom and Elizabeth and John Sherrill, *The Hiding Place* (Grand Rapids, MI: Chosen Books, 2006).

EMPOWERED TO LOVE

Have you ever heard the phrase "love the unlovable"? When you read that, does someone's name or face pop into your mind? Who are the unlovable people in your life? And how can anyone love someone who is unlovable?

Like just about everyone, I have always had people in my life who seem "unlovable." In school there were girls whom I believed had made it their mission in life to make me miserable. There were boys who hurt me. There were teachers whom I thought wanted me to fail. I have other friends who have been hurt in terrible ways by people who were supposed to care for them. The idea of an unlovable person becomes much more real when I hear their stories.

Reading about Corrie ten Boom's life has taught me many things, but this lesson about love is the one I'll never forget. Her father's words to her, "Whenever we cannot love in the old, human way, Corrie, God can give us the perfect way," come to mind when I'm having a difficult time loving someone.

You may have someone in your life who is hard to love. Maybe it's a kid at school or in your neighborhood. Maybe it's a family member. Or maybe you see things in the news that are going on around the world and it's hard to think that people committing terrible acts are humans loved by God.

It's easy for us to say, "You just need to love that person." But actually loving someone is much harder than saying it. It's a comfort to me to know that sometimes it truly is impossible for me to love another person. But that's when God can give me "the perfect way." As He did for Corrie, He can give us the love we need to pass on to others, even the most unlovable.

QUESTIONS

1. Who in your life seems "unlovable"? Why?

2. Have you ever been frustrated when someone told you that you had to love a difficult person? Why? Can you force yourself to love someone?

3. How has God loved the unlovable? How do we know God is loving? (Read 1 John 4:7–10.)

4. Who is someone you are struggling to love? Commit to pray and ask God to give you His perfect love for this person.

WE LOVE BECAUSE HE FIRST
LOVED US.—1 JOHN 4:19

"We must tell them that there is no pit so deep
that He is not deeper still."

BETSIE TEN BOOM
GRATITUDE

Born on August 19, 1885, Elisabeth ten Boom, or "Betsie," was the oldest child in her family. Her brother, Willem, and sisters, Nollie and Corrie, used to run and play outside, while Betsie was forced to sit inside doing needlework because of a condition called pernicious anemia. This meant her body didn't absorb vitamin B-12 properly, so she grew weak and tired easily. While others might have complained, Betsie had a natural gift for gratitude (being thankful) and a desire to make the world around her a beautiful place.

As she got older, she joined her father, Casper, in his shop. She kept his books, recording how much people owed for the watches and clocks her father repaired and calculating expenses. But what she really loved was keeping house, not books. She spent her evenings mending the skirts Corrie ripped while running about and riding her bike around town. Using her skill at sewing, she made all the women in her family silk dresses.

Eventually, Willem and Nollie both married and moved out of the house, and Cornelia ten Boom, Betsie's mother, passed away. This left just Casper, Betsie, and Corrie. They discovered that Corrie was a natural in the shop, while Betsie was gifted at cooking and keeping up with the housework. She served meals not just to her family, but to police officers, neighbors, and friends. Even when food was scarce, Betsie had a knack for making a feast out of a few potatoes. She would place a pot of tulips in the window each spring, hoping for enough sunlight to keep them alive and fill the kitchen with their beauty.

When Germany threatened the ten Boom's country, Holland, the prime minister assured the Dutch people (the name for those from Holland) that there would be no war. But Casper told his daughters this was not true—there would be war, and Holland would fall to the Germans. Betsie and Corrie responded by kneeling next to the piano bench, praying for the people of Holland. To Corrie's surprise, Betsie also prayed for the Germans.

Casper was right—war did come to Holland. As the Germans attacked, the sound of bombs exploding could be heard through their town. One night, Corrie woke to hear Betsie in the kitchen, making a cup of tea. She got up to join her sister. Later, as she went back to her bedroom, she found a piece of shrapnel from a bomb on her pillow, just where her head had been. She suggested to Betsie what might have happened if she hadn't heard her moving in the kitchen. Betsie responded, "There are no 'ifs' in God's world. And no places that are safer than other places. The center of His will is our only safety—oh Corrie, let us pray that we may always know it!"

Gradually, just as in Germany and other occupied countries, the treatment of Jews worsened. As more and more were arrested and sent to concentration camps, Corrie and Betsie knew they must do something. They built a hiding place in Corrie's room behind a wall, and they provided a place to stay for many of their Jewish countrymen and women. Needing to be able to hide their guests at a moment's notice, they had an alarm system installed. Betsie practiced tactics to delay officers at the door so the Jewish guests could hide quickly. They had trial runs, where the alarm would sound during dinnertime and everyone would run and hide to make it appear like only three people were in the home, rather than nine or ten.

In the evenings, Betsie scheduled entertainment for the family and their guests. One guest might play the violin or another play the piano. They would read a play together, with each person reading the lines of a certain character. One guest knew Italian, and he would teach the language to the other people in the home.

When Betsie was fifty-eight, the family's work of hiding Jews was discovered. Soldiers came to the door, and the guests quickly hid in the hiding place. The officers searched through the house, striking Betsie and Corrie on their faces in an attempt to discover where the guests were hidden.

Neither woman revealed the secret, and the family was arrested.

As Corrie saw her fragile sister's swollen lip and bruised cheek, she exclaimed, "Oh Betsie! He hurt you!"

"Yes," Betsie replied. "I feel sorry for him."

They were forced to board a bus and taken to the office of the chief interrogator, whose job it was to discover what exactly the family had done and where the Jews were hidden. He looked at Casper, who was eighty-four years old now, and wondered why he had to be arrested.

"I'd like to send you home, old fellow," he said to Betsie's father. "I'll take your word that you won't cause any more trouble."

"If I go home today," Casper responded, "tomorrow I will open my door again to any man in need who knocks."

Betsie watched as the interrogator looked at her father with anger and sent him back to sit down.

They were transported to a prison, where the men were separated from the women. Betsie and Corrie said goodbye to their father, unaware it was the last time they would see him. They were also separated from one another for four months, the longest they'd ever been apart. While separated, Corrie received word that all the people in the hiding place had been saved. She also learned that their father had died ten days after being arrested. As they left that prison for another one, Betsie and Corrie found each other at a train station and stayed together from then on.

Betsie had been given a Bible, which was forbidden in the camp, and had generously torn the pages out and handed it out, book by book, to the women in her cell. She saw her surroundings as a mission field, full of people who needed to know the love of God.

"What better way could there be to spend our lives?" she asked Corrie.

"Whatever are you talking about?" Corrie responded.

"These young women. . . . Corrie, if people can be taught to hate, they can be taught to love! We must find the way, you and I, no matter how long it takes."

Corrie realized Betsie was talking about the guards, not just the fellow prisoners. She saw the guards, who treated them terribly, as "wounded human beings," desperately in need of love.

Corrie, too, had been given a Bible. Betsie kept it hidden in a cloth bag, tied around her neck and tucked under her clothes. At night, after the day's work, the two sisters held secret prayer meetings around their bunk. More and more women wanted to hear the truth of Scripture and to pray with the sisters.

One day, Corrie learned the identity of the man who had betrayed them from a fellow prisoner. Jan (pronounced "Yon") Vogel was the man's name, and he had made a business of betraying his fellow Dutchmen and women. Corrie was angry, unable to think of much other than this terrible man.

"Betsie, don't you feel anything about Jan Vogel?" she asked her sister. "Doesn't it bother you?"

"Oh yes, Corrie!" Betsie replied. "Terribly! I've felt for him ever since I knew—and pray for him whenever his name comes into my mind. How dreadfully he must be suffering."

Convicted by her sister's words, Corrie silently prayed and forgave Jan Vogel.

Soon the sisters found themselves boarding another train, this time arriving at Ravensbrück, a German concentration camp just for women. When they arrived, they had to cut their hair off, and Corrie was sad to see Betsie's chestnut waves fall to the ground. They slept five to a bed, and it wasn't long before they began gathering these new women for prayer meetings and Bible studies.

One night, the women's faces lit up as Betsie read to them from the words of Paul in Romans 8:35–39:

Who can separate us from the love of Christ? Can affliction or distress or persecution or famine or nakedness or danger or sword? . . . No, in all these things we are more than conquerors through him who loved us. For I am persuaded that neither death nor life, nor angels nor rulers, nor things present nor things to come, nor powers, nor height nor depth, nor any other created thing will be able to separate us from the love of God that is in Christ Jesus our Lord.

These words were especially meaningful to women who faced nakedness each time they had to report for medical inspection. One day as they were in line, waiting to remove their clothes for the humiliating inspection, it occurred to Corrie that Jesus, too, had experienced the humiliation of nakedness when He died on the cross.

"Betsie," she said to her sister, who was in line in front of her, "they took *His* clothes, too."

She heard a small gasp, and Betsie answered, "Oh, Corrie. And I never thanked Him."

Betsie, always weak because of her anemia, had developed a cough that worsened over time. Corrie had smuggled vitamin drops into the camp with her, but she knew the small bottle couldn't last, especially because Betsie insisted on sharing the drops with other women, at times up to twenty-five each day. And yet, each time she needed them, the drops continued to come out. Betsie told Corrie not to try to explain why it was happening, just to accept it as a gift from God.

One problem they couldn't cure was the infestation of fleas in their new barracks, or bunkroom. The fleas covered their bedding and their bodies, biting them at night. When they first discovered them, Corrie was distraught. What could they do about fleas?

Betsie remembered what they had read that morning in 1 Thessalonians 5:16–18:

> Rejoice always, pray constantly, give thanks in everything; for this is God's will for you in Christ Jesus.

"That's it, Corrie!" Betsie exclaimed. "That's His answer. 'Give thanks in all circumstances!' That's what we can do. We can start right now to thank God for every single thing about this new barracks!"

"Such as?" asked Corrie, doubtfully.

Betsie responded with a list of things: the sisters were together, they had a Bible, the room was crowded so more women could hear the good news about Jesus, even the fleas.

"Betsie," said Corrie, "there's no way even God can make me grateful for a flea."

"Give thanks in *all* circumstances," answered Betsie.

The sisters would read the Bible each night, translating it aloud from Dutch to German, then listening as it was passed throughout the barracks in French, Polish, Russian, and Czech. The women were thirsty for the truth and grace of God's Word. And to Betsie and Corrie's shock, the guards never came in and disturbed them. Guards were in every other room but never theirs for some reason.

One day, when Betsie and other women in their barracks were doing their assigned knitting, they had a question about the work and asked a guard to come answer it. But no guard would enter the room; they all refused.

That night, when Corrie returned from her work, Betsie told her she had discovered why the guards never entered and disturbed their Bible study. She explained how no guards would come help them and how one guard finally explained why.

"Because of the fleas!" she proclaimed excitedly. "That's what she said, 'That place is crawling with fleas!'"

Betsie had a soft heart toward her fellow prisoners, but also toward the guards who persecuted them. She wanted them to know that love was greater than hate. She told Corrie that when they were released, they would have a large house with beautiful gardens, and they would use it to help people who had been in the concentration camps. She described the house in such detail, down to the statues in the hall, that it was as if she had been there. But she also had a vision of a camp that was turned into a place to help former guards and those who had treated the prisoners cruelly. She told Corrie they "must tell people what we have learned here. We must tell them that there is no pit so deep that He is not deeper still. They will listen to us, Corrie, because we have been here."

Eventually, Betsie grew so weak and sick that she could no longer move her arms and legs. She died on December 16, 1944, at the age of fifty-nine. It was just fifteen days before Corrie was released from the camp and allowed to return to their home.

Corrie went on to do just what Betsie had said— she told people about their time in the camp and described Betsie's vision of a home where people from the camps could learn to live again. One day, after she had spoken to a group, a woman came up to her and offered the use of her fifty-six-room mansion with extensive gardens. As she described it, down to the floors and statues, Corrie realized it was the house Betsie had envisioned.

Corrie went on to tell this story of God's love to people all over the world, and even though Betsie didn't get to see it, her life inspired many people to set aside their hate and learn instead to love.

SOURCE
Corrie ten Boom and Elizabeth and John Sherrill, *The Hiding Place* (Grand Rapids, MI: Chosen Books, 2006).

EMPOWERED WITH GRATITUDE

Because everything we know about Betsie is from Corrie's memory and perspective, she can seem like she's not fully human—as if she had no flaws. But when we read about her, we know she's the kind of person who, if she could tell her own story, would be quick to point out her own sin and lack of thankfulness. Betsie wasn't perfect, but she was captured by the love of Jesus and wanted everyone else to know that love too.

Betsie had the God-given ability to see the humanity in each person and to empathize with them. (*Empathy* means to understand and feel what another person feels.) She felt badly for the soldier who hit her face, for the man who betrayed her family, and for the guards who persecuted the prisoners. This is not a natural human ability—it's something God has to do in our hearts. The same God who helped Betsy feel empathy can help you with that too. It probably won't be toward a prison guard, but it could be toward a family member or classmate. We understand what others feel when we think about how *we* would feel if we didn't know the love of Jesus.

In many ways, empathy comes from gratitude, which we see repeatedly in Betsie's story. She was so grateful for God's love for her in Jesus that she saw everyone around her with His eyes—as people who needed Him. When we're thankful for God's love for us, we can look around us at friends, neighbors, and family with the same love for them.

God alone can give us the kind of radical gratitude that thanks Him even for fleas. And yet, Betsie knew that God is in control, and she trusted that she could be grateful for whatever He brought her way. Through His power, you can "give thanks in all circumstances."

QUESTIONS

---

1. Are there any things in your life that you have a hard time thanking God for? What are they?

2. If you are in Christ, which means you've trusted Him for salvation and forgiveness of sins, then God is working all things for your good. How does knowing this lead you to be grateful for whatever happens in life?

3. Does being in Christ mean everything that happens will be easy and fun? How does Betsie's life answer that question?

4. Read Matthew 28:20. What was the last thing Jesus said to His disciples and followers before He went back into heaven? That promise is for you too.

5. Pray that you would know that promise deep down in your heart and that it would help you be grateful in all circumstances today.

Rejoice always, pray constantly, give thanks in everything; for this is God's will for you in Christ Jesus.—1 Thessalonians 5:16-18

"A life totally committed to God has nothing to fear, nothing to lose, and nothing to regret."

PANDITA RAMABAI
FEARING GOD, NOT MAN

Pandita Ramabai was an educated Indian woman passionate about Jesus and the treatment of women and girls in her country. As you'll see, the name "Pandita" was a title, like "Teacher" or "Master." So we'll call her what her friends and family called her—Ramabai (pronounced "ram-uh-BYE").

Ramabai's father, Anant Shastri, grew up, like most Indians in the 1800s, believing women could not be taught to read and write. But during his days as a student, he witnessed a woman learning to read and recite Sanskrit, the ancient language of India in which the Hindu religious scriptures and other literature were written. Anant Shastri decided that women and men both should have this knowledge, and he determined to teach his wife to read. His wife did not desire this knowledge, so he gave up the plan. But when she died, he married again. His family did not approve of his desire to teach his wife, so he took her and moved into the jungle, where they raised their family.

It was in this jungle home that Ramabai was born and grew. Her mother taught her to read and write from the Hindu religious texts and folktales, and her father was joined by students and travelers who wanted to learn from his wisdom. By the time she was twelve, Ramabai had memorized eighteen thousand verses from the sacred Hindu texts. It was extremely rare for a young woman to have the education and knowledge she possessed, even for someone of her high caste. (A "caste" was the social and religious group into which you were born. Ramabai was a Brahmin, which means her family was in the highest and most revered caste. This gave them many privileges, but even in the Brahmin caste, the education of women was generally not approved of.)

When she was in her early teens, Ramabai's family lost most of their money and belongings through famine and debt. Because they were in a high caste, they were not trained to work. Ramabai and her older brother and sister had a lot of knowledge, but no skills that would enable them to get jobs. Instead of trying to work, they spent their money and possessions at various sacred places and temples, hoping that by worshiping Hindu gods and bathing in sacred waters they might be freed from the sin and curse they believed was the cause of their poverty and suffering. Rather than buying food, they tried to earn favor from the gods. Ramabai writes, "But nothing came of all this futile effort to please the gods— the stone images remained as hard as ever, and never answered our prayers."

Eventually, both Ramabai's parents and her sister died from disease and starvation. Her older brother was very weak, and the two of them traveled around, walking over four thousand miles, eating whatever they could find, which wasn't much. In their wanderings, Ramabai began to doubt the Hindu religion she had grown up believing. She saw the priests deceiving people and taking their money, and she tested what she had learned.

Gradually, Ramabai began speaking in public about the education of women. Many people were shocked and impressed by her knowledge. A group of "Pandits," a title given to masters of learning, gave her the privilege of being the only woman to be called a "Pandita," or a mistress of learning. She knew the sacred teachings, and she spoke seven of the many languages of India. She eventually rejected the teaching of Hinduism and married a Bengali lawyer. They were happily married for just nineteen months before her husband died of the disease cholera. Before he died, Ramabai gave birth to their daughter, named Manorama, which means "heart's joy."

The death of Ramabai's husband made her an Indian widow. In many countries, being a widow is a sad thing—a woman's husband has died, and she will hopefully be cared for by her family and friends. But in India, being a widow meant something far worse. Because of the religious teachings, people believed the husband's death was his widow's fault. Many widows were cast out of their homes, sometimes forced to live with their own families again, who many times couldn't afford to feed them. Their heads were shaved, they had to give up their pretty clothes and jewelry, and they were treated terribly.

Making matters worse, many of these widows were young girls, as young as five or six years old. That's hard to understand because children shouldn't be married. But the custom was that sometimes young girls would be "married," which was really a form of engagement that couldn't be broken. A girl would go live with her husband's family and be taught by his mother to cook and clean and take care of a home. And then when the girl was older, she would truly become a wife. But when the husband died, she was considered a widow and had to live the rest of her life in suffering and poverty. Many of these girls didn't even understand what marriage was, but they knew they were called "unlucky" and that they must have done something wrong to be treated so badly.

Because Ramabai was educated, she did not suffer in the way of most Indian widows. She continued to speak about educating women, and her desire to learn English and to receive more training to teach girls led her to England.

While there, she also learned about the Christian faith. She and her baby daughter were cared for by women in the Church of England. She asked what made these women different—they cared for the weak and powerless women in their community. Why did they do that? One woman shared with Ramabai the story of Jesus and the Samaritan woman from John 4. She learned that Jesus loved women in a way no one else did and that He was truly the Savior of the world. She eventually gave her life to Jesus and became a Christian. She had seen many good and true ideas about loving others in the ancient Hindu scriptures, but she realized they could not be kept without the grace of God, which, she said, "makes all the difference in the world."

From England, Ramabai and her daughter traveled to America, where she studied early childhood education in order to take teaching knowledge back to India and use it to educate child widows. She found like-minded, helpful friends in the Woman's Christian Temperance Union, an organization of women who worked for the good of women through things like the right to vote and labor laws. Ramabai spoke throughout America, asking people to help her with her dream of educating and caring for child widows. She received the support she needed and returned to India to put her plans into action.

Before she'd left India for England, Ramabai had found friends in other Hindu reformers—people, especially men, who saw the treatment of women as wrong and wanted to do something about it. But she returned a Christian, and there were many who thought it was wrong for her to teach girls about her faith. She opened a home for child widows named "Sharada Sadan" (Abode of Wisdom), where they were clothed, fed, and educated. It was run by Ramabai and a friend, also a Christian. As the girls saw and felt the love of the workers and the way they treated them differently than everyone else had, they began to wonder why. They had never known anyone like Ramabai—what was it about her faith that made her so different? She kept an open door when she prayed and read the Bible in the mornings, and many of the girls and women joined her and heard the good news of God's love for them.

Her old Brahmin friends did not like this, and they tried to make the Sharada Sadan a Hindu home and school. They wanted her to at least shut her door when she read the Bible and prayed. Family members of the girls who were becoming

Christians tried to force them to leave the home. The Indian newspapers wrote terrible things about Ramabai. She didn't care what they wrote about her but was concerned that the school not be shut down. One of the verses that God used to comfort her during this time was John 16:33, where Jesus says:

> "I have told you these things so that in me you may have peace. You will have suffering in this world. Be courageous! I have conquered the world."

Ramabai learned that it was far more important to fear God and love Him than it was to fear and love the opinions of other people. She wrote:

> Last year I happened to read the Life of Amanda Smith. She had been a slave in America, and had been freed. When she was converted [became a Christian], she shouted and said she had been delivered out of bondage twice—once

out of slavery, and once from the slavery
of sin. And I have a right to praise God
too; for I have been first delivered from
the slavery of man's opinions, from the
fear of man which holds so many of my
dear people, and a second time from the
bondage of sin.

A famine struck parts of India, and Ramabai
realized there were many widows who would
starve if they weren't cared for. So she went on
rescue missions, finding girls and bringing them
to the Sharada Sadan to live. She prayed that hundreds
would come to know Jesus personally, and
God worked in many hearts. The girls and women
in the home who were Christians were now telling
the new girls about the love of Christ.

As the number of girls and women grew, they
needed more money and more space. Ramabai
prayed for wisdom and provision, and God supplied.
They planted an orchard with hundreds of
orange, lime, and mango trees so they could sell

the fruit. A vegetable garden provided most of the vegetables for the school. Eventually, they built a new school with many buildings so more and more people could be cared for. Ramabai named it "Mukti," which means "salvation" or "freedom."

Ramabai knew these girls needed to be educated to read and write, but also to learn skills that would allow them to work when they left the school. Her vision was to raise up Christian women who could support themselves and take the gospel and their education throughout India to transform other communities. They were trained to be teachers, nurses, oil-makers, laundry workers, dairy workers, cooks, field workers, weavers, and seamstresses.

Because the girls didn't have the Bible in their language, Ramabai spent years translating it. The love of Christ spread to the workers who built the school and many in the community. Hundreds came to know Jesus and were baptized. In two famines, Ramabai and her coworkers rescued over two thousand girls and women, bringing them to Mukti, where they would be cared for and loved.

Ramabai died in 1922, when she was sixty-three. But her legacy goes on as the work of Mukti Mission continues at the original location and many others. Because of the work God did in and through Ramabai, children, women, and many people with disabilities are cared for and shown the love of Christ still today.

SOURCES

Helen S. Dyer, *Pandita Ramabai: The Story of Her Life* (Sun City Center, FL: Revival Press, 2014).

Pandita Ramaba Sarasvati, *The High Caste Hindu Woman* (Philadelphia: The Jas. B. Rodgers Printing Co., 1887).

www.helpindiakids.org

EMPOWERED TO FEAR GOD

Most of us care more than we would like to about what other people think of us. The Bible calls this the "fear of man," which means we make decisions based on what other people think, instead of what God says. Proverbs 29:25 says, "The fear of mankind is a snare, but the one who trusts in the LORD is protected."

We might not have to deal with fear of man in the way Ramabai did, being threatened with having her school shut down. But we still deal with it every day—when we choose what to wear, what to say, whom to sit by, what jokes to laugh at. It can be so tempting to do what might make us popular or what's easy. People can make life pretty tough when we don't do what they want us to.

How do we combat the fear of man? Ramabai said she experienced freedom from this, and that freedom can only come from fearing God instead of man. The Bible talks over and over about wisdom and knowledge coming from fearing God. What does that mean? It doesn't mean that we should be terrified of God. It means that we see God as being in control of the world, we know His commands, and we desire to live in obedience to Him. When we come to a crossroads and have to choose whether to obey God or follow those who disobey Him, we care about His opinion more than the opinions of those around us.

If Ramabai had feared man more than God, she would never have been able to accomplish what she did. But she trusted God to take care of her and she walked in obedience. The same God who cared and provided for her will do the same for you. Obeying Him won't make Him love you more—He already loves you so much that He sent His Son to die for you! But when we experience that love, it makes us want to obey Him. We know His ways are best because He wants what is good for us.

Our Father loves to empower us to stand firm and honor Him with our lives. Pray now for freedom from the fear of man—He is faithful to help you!

QUESTIONS

1. In what ways are you tempted to make choices according to the fear of man instead of the fear of the Lord?

2. Are you ever jealous when you see people who seem to get away with doing things that you know are wrong? What does Proverbs 23:17–18 say about this?

3. What did Ramabai say was different about Christianity than other religions? (Hint: She said this thing "makes all the difference in the world.")

4. Ramabai became a Christian after hearing the story of Jesus and the Samaritan woman. Read John 4:1–14. What did Jesus offer the woman?

5. It was very unusual for a Jewish man to talk with a Samaritan woman—the Jews looked down upon Samaritans, and men did not take time to talk in this way with women. But Jesus was different. Why do

you think this story meant so much to Ramabai, an Indian woman?

6. Read John 4:28–30 and 39–42. What did the woman do after Jesus spoke with her? How is this like what Ramabai did? How might God want you to do the same thing?

THE FEAR OF MANKIND IS A SNARE, BUT THE ONE WHO TRUSTS IN THE LORD IS PROTECTED.
—PROVERBS 29:25

"Why was I here? There was no answer but the simplest, most elemental: Jesus Christ. To obey Him, to present Him."

ELISABETH ELLIOT
OBEDIENCE

Elisabeth Howard was born on December 21, 1926, in Brussels, Belgium, where her parents were serving as missionaries. By the time she turned one year old, they had moved to Germantown, Pennsylvania, outside Philadelphia. She was the oldest of six kids, having four younger brothers and one younger sister.

Elisabeth spent time at a boarding school in Orlando, Florida, and then chose to attend Wheaton College in Illinois, where she studied Greek. Her plan was to use knowledge of classical Greek in missionary work after college by translating the Bible into new languages. In school, she was part of a mission fellowship organization, along with other students interested in being missionaries. She met a fellow student named Jim Elliot, and while she tried to pretend she wasn't interested in him, she very much was. Jim, like Elisabeth, was devoted to Jesus and planned to be a missionary after college. They decided to trust the Lord to bring them together after college if that was His plan.

Both Jim and Elisabeth ended up in the South American country of Ecuador after college, but in different places. Eventually, they began working together with the Quichua tribe, and they were married in 1953. Their daughter, Valerie, was born in Ecuador in 1955.

The Elliots worked with three other couples, sharing the gospel with Quichuas and doing translation work. One of the men they worked with, Nate Saint, was a pilot. He would fly over the jungles and make drops of food and supplies to the missionaries living in different areas.

The Quichua people had told the missionaries about the Waorani tribe, or what they called the "Auca" (a Quichua word for "savage") tribe that lived in the jungle. No outsiders had ever made contact with the Waorani and lived to tell about it. The people in this tribe were known for spearing—taking their long, sharp spears and throwing them to kill anyone who approached.

The Waorani had never heard the gospel, and the missionaries hoped to one day be able to tell them the good news about Jesus. There were just a couple of problems: (1) No one knew how to find them, since they lived deep in the jungle, and (2) even if they did find them, they would surely be killed.

One day when Nate Saint was flying over the jungle, he spotted some huts that belonged to the Waoranis. He and the other missionaries were thrilled, and they devised a plan to tie a bucket from the plane using string. They then flew over the settlement and dropped down gifts in the bucket.

This went on for some time, and then the four men of the group, along with another missionary named Roger, decided it was time to meet the Waorani. On January 3, 1956, the five men flew in and set up a tree house on a beach close to the settlement, and then they waited for the people to come. They waited for three days, and then three members of the Waorani tribe—two women and one man—came to the beach. They spent the day with Jim and the other men, inspecting the plane and the other foreign objects they had brought. They couldn't communicate with each other, but the visit was friendly. Then the three walked back into the jungle, leaving the five men hoping they would come back soon.

Two days later, more members of the Waorani tribe came to the beach, but this time they weren't friendly. They speared the five missionaries, leaving their bodies on the beach.

When word of their deaths came to Elisabeth and the other wives, along with video footage of their first meeting with the Waorani, the women did not see their husbands' deaths as meaningless, and they didn't seek revenge. They knew these men died for a purpose. Elisabeth later wrote, "The fact that Jesus Christ died for all makes me interested in the salvation of all, but the fact that Jim loved and died for the [Waorani] intensifies my love for them."

She continued her work, understanding that her obedience to God was the same as the five men who died—they were doing what they believed God wanted them to do. As she lived on in their home, she later wrote, "Obedience, if it is a good reason for dying, is just as good a reason for living. . . . I did the things that presented themselves to me as duties each day, and in the doing of these I learned to know God a little better."

One day, word came that two Waorani women had left their homes and were nearby. Elisabeth went with guides to meet them, and they came back with her. At first, they couldn't communicate, but soon Nate Saint's sister, Rachel, came with a girl named Dayuma. Dayuma was Waorani, but she hadn't lived with the tribe for many years. She was able to communicate with the two women, Mankamu and Mintaka. All of them lived together until Mankamu and Mintaka decided it was time they return to their tribe. They asked Elisabeth to come with them.

"But your people speared my husband. They will spear me," Elisabeth told them.

They answered, "We will say, 'Here is our mother. . . . We love her. She is good.'"

So Elisabeth prayed and asked God if she should go with them. The dangers were obvious, but what of her duty? She wrote, "If a duty is clear, the dangers surrounding it are irrelevant." In other words, no amount of danger should keep us from obeying God.

Dayuma had asked her people why they speared the men on the beach. They told her they believed the men were cannibals, but they also believed lies one of their fellow Waorani had told them. As she told them about the foreigners' kindness, they realized they had killed them for nothing. So Elisabeth did go, along with Valerie. They were joined by Rachel Saint, who was working on understanding their language.

When she decided to go, Elisabeth had peace because she, Valerie, Rachel, and even the Waorani were in God's hands. She wrote that, "Because I could call Him Father, I had nothing to fear."

There were fifty-six members of the Waorani tribe in the village they went to, only seven of whom were adult men. They lived in a grouping of small huts with no walls—just woven palm roofs supported by poles. Quickly, the men built a hut for Elisabeth and Valerie and gave Rachel an addition to an existing hut. There was no furniture—only hammocks. Valerie's bed was made of logs covered with flattened bamboo, while Elisabeth slept, worked on translation, and even cooked from her hammock.

They grew accustomed to sweat bees landing on their food and gnats swarming around their faces. One night, Elisabeth found a snake coiled up by Valerie's head while she slept. Spider monkeys were both food and friends. One day, Elisabeth returned from being out of her hut to discover a woolly spider monkey had eaten her whole week's supply of fresh beef, but had thoughtfully "replaced" the beef by dropping a washcloth in her pot of soup.

The men hunted monkeys, squirrels, toucans, and macaws with blowguns (tubes that shot darts). They hunted larger game, like wild hogs, with their spears. Fish were speared and caught with nets. Elisabeth ate whatever was offered, also learning to cook her own food when possible.

Valerie spent her days playing with the Waorani children, sharing her picture books and teaching them to color with crayons. She loved to swim in the nearby river, where the older boys would jump, splash, and scare one another by shouting "Anaconda!" or "Electric eel!" (Both of which were present in the jungle rivers, along with alligators and piranhas.) Valerie's favorite playthings, however, were a large hunting knife and fire. As a five-year-old, she dug holes, chopped weeds, peeled plantains, and built fires. She understood the language better than her mother and enjoyed her carefree jungle life.

Meanwhile, Elisabeth spent every moment trying to understand the Waorani language. She had index cards and a tape recorder, and she took notes constantly, hoping to learn what the people were saying and to imitate their speech. At first, the Waorani could not comprehend that anyone didn't understand them—they assumed Elisabeth and Rachel knew everything they said, but just acted like they didn't. But eventually they saw the truth and called the foreigners "earless." They even thought for a time that Elisabeth couldn't understand them because her hair covered her ears. Trying to be helpful, they suggested she shave the hair in front of her ears so she could hear. This was a bit much for her, but she did tuck the hair behind her ears to prove that this wasn't the problem.

Living with the Waorani taught Elisabeth what being a servant truly meant. They did not see her as smarter or more capable than they were; quite the opposite, actually. Her inability to understand them and to do the tasks that filled their days—hunting, preparing food, making hammocks—could have caused them to disdain her. Instead, they treated her as an equal. When an older woman commanded her to go get a pot of water, she realized servanthood meant taking the form of a younger Waorani woman, rather than telling the older Waorani women what to do.

While she was understanding more of what it meant to be a missionary, never did she question her decision to be one. She wrote that she was obeying God, doing the thing He meant her to do, just as He meant for other people to be fishermen, housewives, architects, and other things. "The role seemed incidental," she wrote. "The goal was all-important."

And what was the goal? To give the Waorani what they truly needed—what everyone needs: Jesus Christ. During her years with the Waorani, Elisabeth learned more about her need for Jesus, writing:

. . . they do not need Christ more than I do, for we are all of us sheep who have turned every one to his own way. If I know who the Shepherd is and how to find Him, it is surely my duty to do what I can to point other sheep to Him.

Elisabeth and Valerie spent two years with the Waorani, ending the eight years Elisabeth spent as a missionary in Ecuador. Moving back to America, Valerie started school, grew up, married a pastor, and homeschooled their eight children. And Elisabeth started writing. She wrote and published twenty-four books.

Many people criticized Elisabeth for going to live with the people who had killed her husband, and even more for taking her young daughter with her. They were right about the risk, but they didn't understand she was obeying God. Some people think that if you're obeying God, nothing bad will happen to you. Elisabeth knew that wasn't

true—her husband had died while obeying God.
She wrote:

> I found peace in the knowledge that I
> was in the hands of God. Not in the con-
> fidence that I was not going to be killed.
> Not in any false sense of security that
> God would protect me, any more than
> He protected my husband, the four mis-
> sionaries, or Honorio [a Quichua man
> who was speared] from the wooden
> lances. Simply in knowing that He held
> my destiny in His two hands, and what
> He did was right.

In the end, the Waorani people heard about
Jesus, and many began following His path, putting away their spears. Rachel Saint stayed with
them until her death, and other missionaries
came to work with them as well.

Elisabeth married again—a man named
Addison Leitch, who passed away from cancer
four years after they were married. God brought

Lars Gren into her life later, and they were married until she died in 2015 at the age of eighty-nine.

SOURCE

Elisabeth Elliot, *The Savage My Kinsman* (Ann Arbor, MI: Servant Books, 1981).

EMPOWERED TO OBEY

I remember hearing stories about Elisabeth Elliot and other missionaries when I was growing up and thinking, "I could never be like them. They're like super-Christians, and I'm just normal." But the truth is that she was just as normal as me and you. She did what God put in her heart to do, and she was faithful to obey in the things right in front of her. As exciting as it seems to live in the jungle, most of her days were full of writing on note cards and cooking for her daughter. That doesn't seem all that glamorous.

Obeying God isn't always full of adventure and excitement, and it's rarely easy. It might not lead to fame and money and nice possessions. But it's always worth the cost. Always.

The same God who held Elisabeth and Valerie in His hands holds you as well. If you've trusted Christ, your Father is holding you right now. And He won't ever let you go. He carries you as you go to school, talk to neighbors, work, spend money, play sports, practice instruments—whatever you do.

When something sad happens to someone you love, He's holding you. When you're sick, He's holding you. When you're confused about the next step you should take, He's holding you. When you're afraid, He's holding you. This faithful, loving God can be trusted, and He deserves to be obeyed. When you trust Him, no matter how hard it is to obey, He's holding you and helping you by the power of the Holy Spirit.

And when you fail to obey, He loves you, forgives you, and is holding you then too.

QUESTIONS

1. Read John 14:15–17. What does Jesus say we will do if we love Him? Whom does Jesus say the Father will send to help us obey?

2. On an ordinary day, do you think about obeying God's commands? Whom do you think about obeying? (Hint: Obeying the authorities in your life is a way of obeying God, as long as they aren't telling you to do something against God's commands.)

3. What are God's commands? Look up the following verses and see what you can discover:

- 2 John 1:6
- Matthew 22:37–40

4. When Elisabeth Elliot was trying to figure out if God wanted her to go to live with the Waorani tribe, she read the Bible. Do you look for God's direction through His Word or through other things? What things?

5. What is one way you can obey God this week by loving Him and loving others? Pray now that the Holy Spirit will help you obey.

6. When you don't obey, did you know God will forgive you? Here's a sample prayer to pray:

> *Father, I'm so sorry I disobeyed You by _____. Please forgive me. Thank You for sending Jesus to live and die for me so that I don't have to be punished for my sin. Thank You for Your forgiveness. Help me to obey You. I love You. Amen.*

God doesn't want us to live life feeling guilty—He wants us to have the joy of forgiveness. Jesus lived a perfect life in our place, always obeying, so that we don't have to be perfect in order to know God. So rejoice now, knowing you've been forgiven!

"IF YOU LOVE ME,
YOU WILL KEEP MY
COMMANDS. AND I WILL
ASK THE FATHER, AND HE
WILL GIVE YOU ANOTHER
COUNSELOR TO BE WITH
YOU FOREVER." —JOHN
14:15-16

"But O that I could dwell on & delight in
[Jesus] alone above every other object!"

PHILLIS WHEATLEY
USING YOUR TALENTS

In 1761, a young African girl found herself separated from her home, her family, and everything familiar. Suddenly captured and placed on a ship bound for America, this seven-year-old was surrounded by the sickness and death common to the terrible journey across the Atlantic Ocean aboard a slave ship. Many did not survive the voyage, but this young girl did.

What must she have thought when she arrived in Boston Harbor, immediately greeted with all new sights, sounds, and smells? She would have seen carriages drawn by great horses, large brick homes, print shops, blacksmiths, taverns, men and boys selling fish. No doubt she was confused and scared. The next step in her journey was to be sold to the highest bidder—someone who wanted her to work as a house slave. The people who bought this young girl were John and Susanna

Wheatley. They named her "Phillis," after the ship *Phillis* that had brought her across the ocean.

Phillis went to live with the Wheatleys, but we don't know a lot about her life as a child. She probably worked in their home, helping with household chores. But we also know she learned to read and write quickly, most likely taught by her master's daughter, Mary. With the Wheatley family, she attended church and went to other social gatherings in town. She studied the Bible and ancient Greek literature. She read the Boston news and knew what was going on around the city.

And there was a lot happening in Boston. In her early years in America, the famous preacher George Whitefield came to Boston, and many people followed Jesus because of his teaching. Phillis' master and mistress knew Whitefield because he would preach in their church and attend dinners with their social circle when he was in Boston, so Phillis probably had the opportunity to know him as well.

In fact, she was so inspired by Whitefield that she took out her inkwell and her feather quill pen and wrote an elegy—or a funeral poem—to honor him when he died. People loved her poem so much that it was published in newspapers and passed around both in the American colonies and in England. Phillis was just a teenager when news of her talent for poetry began to spread. She continued to write many other elegies, as well as poems on other subjects.

But it wasn't just George Whitefield's visits and death that made news in Boston. This port city was the focus of all the colonies in the early 1770s. America was on the edge of war with England's King George III and the British Parliament requiring the colonies to pay taxes that many colonists thought were unfair. A tax on tea resulted in what we now know as the Boston Tea Party. This act of rebellion led the British to further invade Boston. Phillis grew into adulthood in the middle of a city filled with tension. Many feared they were heading for war with Parliament and the Continental Congress unable to reach an agreement.

In the midst of this, Phillis continued to write. She wrote about events and people from Boston and surrounding areas. She wrote about King George III and a desire for peace. She wrote about her faith in God and the freedom He gives.

Phillis wrote so much and so well that her master decided to have her writing published. This would have been very unusual. Many white colonists at the time thought slaves should not be allowed to learn to read and write. They certainly didn't encourage it. They were afraid slaves would learn too much and would then rise up against their masters and fight for freedom. There were also many people who believed Africans were not as smart as white people. They believed slavery was okay because they thought the people they were buying and selling were not fit for anything other than manual labor.

And then add the fact that Phillis was not just a slave, but also a woman. Many women in the American colonies could not read or write. Many who could, read only what was necessary. They certainly weren't reading ancient literature or modern poetry.

Phillis was unique. She had a gift and love for poetry, and she used it well. But there were always obstacles to getting others to see and believe her talent. Before she could have her book published, Phillis had to sit before eighteen of Boston's most important and well-known men, who gathered to determine whether she had truly written the poems her master claimed she had. These men included John Hancock, famous for his signature on the Declaration of Independence, and Thomas Hutchinson, the governor of Massachusetts. We don't know what they made her do—perhaps quote poetry from other famous poets or translate something from Latin—but whatever the questions were, Phillis answered them well enough that these men all agreed to write and sign a letter that was included in the front of her book, telling publishers, buyers, and readers that Phillis was the author. Without this letter, few people would have believed a young slave girl could have written it.

Even so, Phillis found much of the support for her writing across the Atlantic Ocean in England. When she was twenty-two, she traveled to London for health reasons and to meet some of the men and women who had supported her writing. Perhaps it was hard climbing aboard a ship, remembering what her first experience crossing the Atlantic had been like. We don't know what she felt, but we do know that she enjoyed her time in London. She was guided around the city by a man named Granville Sharp, who was passionate about seeing slavery ended and slaves set free. Probably because of her time in London and changing laws there, when Phillis returned home, her master, John Wheatley, gave her freedom.

No longer a slave, she remained in the Wheatley home for a few more years as a companion and help to the family.

It might be easy to read her poetry and think she was happy as a slave. She was given many opportunities to learn about God and to make a name for herself as a poet. But nothing was truly hers—even her name was not her own. She lived much of her life as someone else's property. But what Phillis learned as she studied the Bible was that freedom is important to God. She wrote to a friend, the Native American pastor Samson Occom, that "in every human Breast [or heart], God has implanted a Principle, which we call Love of Freedom; it is impatient of Oppression [cruel treatment], and pants for Deliverance."

Her poetry shows that Phillis understood the American colonists' thirst for freedom from what they saw as England's cruel treatment. As a slave, she knew what it was like to long for freedom. But she also saw that many colonists were hypocrites—they said they believed in liberty and justice for all, but that "all" didn't include slaves.

As a woman and a slave, Phillis didn't have the freedom to speak out against slavery on the street or in the newspapers. But what she did have was a talent for poetry. In some of her poems, it seems she's writing about American freedom, but she adds comments about justice for those enslaved, like her. In one poem, titled "On the Death of General Wooster," she writes in the voice of this Patriot general:

> But how, presumptuous shall we hope
>   to find
> Divine acceptance with th' Almighty
>   mind—
> While yet (O deed Ungenerous!) they
>   disgrace
> And hold in bondage Afric's blameless
>   race?
> Let Virtue reign—And Thou accord our
>   prayers

> Be victory our's, and generous freedom
>   theirs.

The language is a bit hard to understand for our modern time. This poem is written as though General Wooster—an honored white man—is speaking, saying that it is prideful to assume God will give the victory in the Revolutionary War to a people who hold Africans as slaves. Instead, he prays that God might give them victory and also give the slaves freedom.

Even when Phillis wasn't writing about slavery and freedom, God used her talent to display to the world that every person is created in His image and is equal in His sight. Before they read her writing, many white Europeans and Americans believed Africans could not be educated—that they were not as smart as white people and could never create the same kind of art and literature. But reading the poems and letters Phillis wrote caused many of these people to rethink their views of slavery. Her writing also inspired other Africans and women to use their own talents.

More than any other freedom, though, Phillis believed that serving Christ was "the most perfect freedom." She used her gifts to point others to Him and to the hope we have in being with Him for eternity.

Phillis died from childbirth complications when she was in her early thirties. She was poor and had struggled to get more of her poems published. The war had changed many things in the colonies. After her death, her writing received more attention. Today, a statue of Phillis Wheatley stands in Boston, honoring her talent and her courage in using it to seek freedom for all.

SOURCE

Vincent Carretta, *Phillis Wheatley: Biography of a Genius in Bondage* (Atlanta: University of Georgia Press, 2011).

EMPOWERED WITH TALENT

When I was young, my dream was to be an Olympic gymnast. Well actually, first it was to be the lady who sold popcorn at the grocery store so that I could eat all the popcorn, but later it was to be a gymnast. And then a writer. Then a teacher. My dreams changed a lot.

Maybe you're the same way. You're probably starting to see certain talents you have—maybe artistic talents or an interest in math or science. Maybe you're a good athlete, a gifted musician, or you love to read. And maybe you're not sure what you're good at. That's totally normal. I'm thirty-five and still figuring out some of these things.

Most of my childhood dreams revolved around, well, *me.* I wanted the glory of a gold medal or the tastiness of that popcorn. I didn't think much about using my talents to serve and help others. You might struggle with the same thing.

Or, perhaps you do think about using your talents for God and others, but only in the distant future when you're older.

The talents you have are no mistake; they are a present from your Creator. And they're not just there for the future; they're for you to use and practice and grow in right now. He made you uniquely for a purpose—to enjoy Him and to help others enjoy Him too! Have you ever thought about how to do that right now, right where you are? In school? In sports? In church? In your neighborhood?

We have no way of knowing what Phillis Wheatley's life would have been like if she hadn't been kidnapped and sold into slavery. We don't even know what her real name was. But we do know that God shaped her life and gave her a talent that enabled her to show people that all men and women are created equal.

The same God who gave Phillis a talent to write poetry and empowered her to use that talent for good can empower you to use your talents also.

Start asking Him for opportunities and strength to do that now.

QUESTIONS

---

1. Phillis believed true freedom is found in Jesus Christ. But she also believed every man and woman should be free from slavery and cruel treatment. How did she use her poetry to seek spiritual and physical freedom for others?

2. Read Psalm 139:13–14. What do these verses say about God? What do they say about humans?

3. God shaped you in your mother's womb, and every part of you is a wonderful work of God's creation. What are some of the talents He has given you?

4. What are some of your dreams—for this year and for the future?

5. Why is it tempting to use our talents to bring glory and fame to ourselves? How do you see this happening in the world around you?

6. How can you use your dreams and talents to serve others and bring glory to God? Ask God to shape your heart and give you a desire for *His* glory.

FOR WE ARE HIS
WORKMANSHIP, CREATED
IN CHRIST JESUS FOR
GOOD WORKS, WHICH
GOD PREPARED AHEAD OF
TIME FOR US TO DO.
-EPHESIANS 2:10

"I saw that my injury was not a tragedy but a gift God was using to help me conform to the image of Christ, something that would mean my ultimate satisfaction, happiness—even joy."

JONI EARECKSON TADA
LIVING ABUNDANTLY

Joni (pronounced like "Johnny," after her dad) grew up in Maryland in the 1950s and '60s. Her family had a ranch where they kept horses. Joni's horse was named Tumbleweed, and together they won many ribbons and horse show awards. She could ride him fast, breezing over jumps and rails.

Joni's childhood was full of activity. In high school, she was the captain of her lacrosse team and was always surrounded with friends. One year, she went to Young Life camp—a Christian camp for high schoolers. There, she heard about "the abundant life" from John 10:10. She said, "In my immature mind, the abundant life meant I'd lose weight or have new popularity and dates at school, lots of friends, and good grades." Joni thought she loved Jesus, but in her day-to-day life, she just didn't think she needed Him. She was doing pretty good on her own.

The summer before her last year of high school, when she was seventeen, Joni went swimming in the nearby Chesapeake Bay. She dove into the cool water and then felt her head hit something hard. She discovered she was lying facedown on the sand in the water. She struggled but couldn't lift herself up. Suddenly she heard a voice. Her sister Kathy was calling her name, asking if she was all right. Kathy pulled her up and onto a raft that a nearby swimmer brought over. She cried out to Kathy that she couldn't move. Kathy was holding Joni's hands, but she couldn't feel them.

Soon Joni was being rushed to the hospital. Joni could feel nothing in her arms, legs, or torso. But she thought the numbness would soon fade and she would regain feeling.

Eventually, after a series of surgeries, a doctor delivered the crushing news: Joni had total quadriplegia. She would never walk again, and she might not regain use of her hands. She spent her days lying in something called a Stryker frame—a hanging "canvas sandwich." After lying there for two hours on her back, nurses would come and flip her over to spend two hours on her stomach, then return to her back, and so on.

After weeks of wondering why this had happened to her, a friend shared with her the promise of Romans 8:28: "All things work together for the good of those who love God, who are called according to his purpose." Joni was convinced that God had allowed this in her life so that He could show His power through healing her. She knew that He would perform a miracle and she would regain the ability to walk.

But the weeks turned into months and years, and still she couldn't walk. She struggled with depression, saying, "I had absolutely no idea of how I could find purpose or meaning in just existing day after day—waking, eating, watching TV, sleeping."

Yet God faithfully brought Joni friends and books to point to the truth about God from the Bible. She realized that Jesus knew what she was feeling. He had been paralyzed on the cross, unable to move his arms and legs. He knew her deepest pain and sorrow. Before the accident, she hadn't thought she needed Jesus. Now, she was aware of how much He cared for her.

And He brought her new joys. She learned to feed herself again and to use a motorized wheelchair. She had wheelchair races with a friend from the rehabilitation center where she was staying. In one race, they went too quickly and whipped around a corner where Joni ran into a nurse who was carrying a tray of medicine. The next instant, Joni's chair was pinning the nurse to the wall, and the floor was covered in medicine bottles. After that, the workers made Joni drive more slowly.

But it wasn't just wheelchair races and feeding herself that brought Joni joy. Before her accident, she had been a talented artist. One day, her therapist suggested she try drawing a picture on a piece of clay. How could she draw without the use of her hands? She held a stylus in her mouth. Chris, the therapist, encouraged her, telling her she had great talent. She began to practice drawing and painting and discovered she could be even better at it after her accident than she had been before.

When she looked around, though, it was hard not to compare her life and her body with the people surrounding her. Eventually, she realized that was the case for everyone—we're all tempted to compare ourselves with friends, classmates, neighbors. She learned to thank God that she was "his workmanship, created in Christ Jesus" (Ephesians 2:10). She started to thank Him for who she was and for what she could and even *couldn't* do.

And she started to get a glimpse of what an abundant life really is. Colossians 3:2 says, "Set your minds on things above, not on earthly things." Joni says, "Since I could see that one day [in the New Creation] I'd have a renewed body, it became easier for me to focus my desires on heavenly, eternal things. I had already lost temporal things, the use of my earthly body, so it was easy to accept this truth. Although 'condemned' to a wheelchair, I knew one day I'd be free of it." She told a friend, "I'm beginning to see the chair more as a tool than as a tragedy. I believe God is going to teach me something more about this!"

The abundant life wasn't all those things she had cared about before she was injured. If that had been the abundant life, then it wouldn't have been available to her now. Her injury would mean she couldn't have that kind of life. But Jesus didn't just come to offer life in abundance to people who were popular, rich, smart, or athletic. He came for everyone—young and old, weak and strong, healthy and sick. We're all desperate for Him.

For Joni, the abundant life God had for her included her talent for art. One day when she was twenty-three, a Christian businessman was in Joni's father's office and noticed a drawing hanging on his wall. When he learned that Joni had drawn it, he decided to organize an art exhibit for her. They took several of her drawings to a local restaurant for what Joni thought would be a small gathering. But when she arrived, there were TV cameras and a large crowd gathered. Everyone loved her art and wanted to know how she drew her pictures.

This led to more TV interviews, including an appearance on the national morning program *The Today Show*. She got to talk to over twenty million people about her art and her faith in Christ. Soon, people started writing to Joni, asking how they could purchase some of her art. She wrote up a paper that she handed out at art shows, explaining how she created her pictures and talking about her faith in Jesus. People would stop to talk with her, and she was able to tell them about the power of God. She knew God had given her this gift for drawing so that she could glorify Him. She has now created around one hundred fifty paintings and drawings, including well-known pieces like "Rock of Ages" and "Green Pastures."

Now, Joni is married to Ken Tada, and she has written over forty-five books. Her first book, *Joni: An Unforgettable Story*, has been translated into fifty languages. She also has a ministry called "Joni and Friends" that helps people with disabilities and provides wheelchairs to those who can't afford them.

Life since her accident hasn't been easy. But it's been abundant, because she's been living for the One who came to give her true purpose and joy. Her heart is set on things above, where her Savior is. And one day, she'll run to Him.

SOURCE

Joni Eareckson Tada, *Joni: An Unforgettable Story* (Grand Rapids, MI: Zondervan, 1976).

EMPOWERED WITH ABUNDANT LIFE

Before reading this chapter, had you ever heard anyone talk about "the abundant life"? Did you have any thoughts about what it might look like?

Other words for abundant are *plentiful* and *huge*. An abundant life is a life of lots, not little. It's a life of big, not small. It seems like it might be a "dream come true" kind of life.

You've probably had ideas of what your own abundant life might be. It might include some of the following: A big house. The most stylish clothes. Lots of pets. Popularity. Great vacations. Captain of a sports team. Talented musician. Fame.

We all have a vision of the abundant life—what we think would be the best life for us. Sometimes we see other people, maybe even friends, who have the life we want. Seeing that can cause us to resent our friends who have those things. If a friend is a better athlete, your jealousy might keep you from cheering for her. If another friend's family has a bigger house and goes on amazing vacations, you might start to complain about your own home and family.

You might be thinking something like, "I know in my mind that Jesus is better and life with Him is better, but I want these other things so much." I get that, because it's an ongoing battle for every Christian. You're not alone.

God taught Joni what true abundance is through an extremely difficult circumstance. In my life, He's used smaller things—friends who have suffered, injuries, hard friendships—to show me that He is better than anything. It could be the same for you. When we lose something we love, sometimes He's taking away an idol—something that has been more important to us than He is. But He loves us so much and He created us to be happiest when we are living for Him. So sometimes He takes things away so we will see how wonderful He truly is.

Through her injury, God shaped Joni's life in ways she never could have predicted. But He was faithful every day, and He'll continue to be faithful to you too. Life with Him truly is abundant.

QUESTIONS

---

1. When Jesus talked about the abundant life, He said He was a shepherd who came so that His sheep could have life in abundance (John 10:10). What did He say right after that, in verse 11?

2. Do you ever worry that the world's idea of abundance might actually be better than God's? What are some things that have been part of your "dream life"?

3. Read Matthew 6:19–21. What does Jesus say about the things we love in this world?

4. Does it encourage you to read that God brought new joys to Joni after He took other things away? How does it help you trust and love God more?

SET YOUR MINDS ON
THINGS ABOVE, NOT ON
EARTHLY THINGS.
-COLOSSIANS 3:2

"This is my story, this is my song,
Praising my Savior all the day long."

FANNY CROSBY
KINDNESS

Fanny (short for Frances) was born in 1820 in a small town in New York. She was a healthy baby until she was six weeks old, when she caught a cold that caused her eyes to become swollen. Her family doctor was away, so they called a stranger who said he had medical experience. This man recommended a treatment that apparently ruined Fanny's sense of sight and left her blind.

Fanny didn't let her blindness hold her back— she could climb trees, ride horses, climb stone fences, and play everything the other children played. She grew up in a cottage near a tiny brook, where she loved sitting on a large rock under a grapevine and an apple tree, listening to bees, locusts, crickets, birds, and the rippling of the water. When she was very small, she had a tiny lamb that followed her through fields and napped with her under a large oak tree.

From a young age, Fanny loved poetry and music. She would sit and listen to people singing in different churches in town, and she loved writing her own poems. When she was around eight or nine years old, she wrote this poem:

Oh, what a happy soul I am,
    Although I cannot see,
I am resolved that in this world
    Contented I will be.

How many blessings I enjoy
    That other people don't!
To weep and sigh because I'm blind
    I cannot nor I won't.

While she was content to be blind, there *was* one thing that blindness kept her from: school. Fanny longed to learn like other children but could not attend school because there was no way for her to study in a traditional classroom. One night when she was eleven, she laid in her room and prayed, "Dear Lord, please show me how I can learn like other children." Then she trusted that God would give her a way to gain an education.

She waited four long years after praying that prayer, still trusting that God would provide a way. Just before she turned fifteen, He answered her prayer. Fanny left home to live at the New York Institute for the Blind in New York City.

Leaving home was bittersweet—she would finally be going to school, but she had to leave her family behind. She adjusted to her boarding school, quickly making friends with the students and teachers. She loved learning but struggled with math. Eventually she had a teacher who insisted Fanny simply couldn't learn math and worked it out for her to study something else instead. (If only I had had that teacher when *I* was in school.)

She continued writing poetry, often staying up into the early morning hours. Because of her blindness, she could not just sit and write it on paper, crossing out wrong words and replacing them with better ones. Instead, she would "write" the entire poem in her head, turning the words around in her mind and getting it just right before asking a friend to write it down for her.

Fanny was so gifted at writing poetry that she had several books of poems published. When the first one was being put together, she was asked to have her picture taken for the book. Unlike today, when we can take a picture on a cell phone in one second, the process of having a picture taken when Fanny was a young woman required her to sit perfectly still and pose for four minutes. Even as an adult, Fanny was known for being energetic and having trouble sitting still. Her friends thought having her picture taken would be impossible for her. She writes, "The idea that I, the restless Fanny Crosby as they all knew me, would be obliged to sit still so long—well that was indeed very funny. As a result I burst into a laugh right in the midst of my 'sitting,'" and the photographer had to start over again.

Having finished her studies at the institute, Fanny stayed on as a teacher. Because of her poetry, when she was twenty-three, Fanny was invited to deliver a poem before Congress in Washington, DC. She and other representatives from her school traveled there to try to convince lawmakers that every state needed a school for the blind. But she didn't just meet congressmen and senators during her life. Fanny also got to know three presidents of the United States: John Tyler, James K. Polk, and Grover Cleveland. She knew Cleveland when she was thirty-five and he was just seventeen. He worked at her school and would often sit and write her poems down for her as she composed them in her mind.

While she had grown up attending church, she was more concerned with her work than she was with God. But when she was twenty-nine, there was a terrible cholera outbreak in New York City, sadly leading to the deaths of several residents of the institute where she lived. As a friend of hers was dying, he asked if Fanny would meet him in heaven. She said she would, but then began to wonder if she actually should have said that. Was she truly a Christian—a follower of Christ?

Later, in a church service she attended, the congregation sang a song with the line, "Here Lord, I give myself away." She later said that when she heard that line, "for the first time I realized that I had been trying to hold the world in one hand and the Lord in the other." She gave her life to Jesus and became a Christian. But she said her growth in grace was slow . . . she didn't change overnight. She had to keep giving her life to the Lord daily. What she learned, though, was that nothing in this world compares to Jesus. She wrote a song called "Give Me Jesus," which includes this verse:

> Take the world, but give me Jesus,
> All its joys are but a name,
> But His love abideth ever,
> Through eternal years the same.

After she gave her life to Jesus, she began using her talent for poetry to write hymns. She was gifted musically—she played the guitar, piano, organ, and harp—and it was natural that she began putting her words to music. By the end of her life, Fanny had written at least eight thousand hymns. In fact, some of the people who published hymnbooks were concerned about including too many hymns written by one person, so she used pseudonyms (fake names) for some of her hymns. She wrote so many that she even forgot some of them. On more than one occasion, she heard a hymn being sung and asked who wrote it, only to be told that *she* was the writer.

Her songs were known all over the United States, and many were sung in other parts of the world. Two of her most famous songs, "Blessed Assurance" and "God Be with You Till We Meet Again," were even used as a code by members of the British Soldiers' Christian Association. When they passed each other, one soldier would say, "Four-nine-four, boys," to which the other soldier would reply, "Six further on." This was because in their hymnbook, one of these hymns was number 494, and the other was 500.

Fanny was deeply concerned for hurting and lonely men and women to know the hope that comes only from Jesus, and she wrote many words that pointed them to that hope. She wrote, "Some of the most gratifying memories of my life center about testimonies of those whom I have been enabled to help by words of cheer toward better things than those of this world."

Fanny fervently believed that:

> Kindness in this world will do much to help others, not only to come into the light, but to grow in grace day by day. There are many timid souls whom we jostle morning and evening as we pass them by; but if only the kind word were spoken they might become fully persuaded [to follow Jesus].

For someone who was so well-known by presidents and "important" people of her day, Fanny knew that every person mattered. At one point during his presidency, President Polk had made an official visit to the New York Institute for the Blind, but later he came by himself unannounced one day and spent time walking and talking with Fanny. In the middle of her conversation with the president, Fanny recognized the voice of a favorite older woman who had been a maid at the home. Knowing she might not talk with this woman again for months, she asked President Polk to excuse her so she could go greet her friend. When she returned, she apologized to him for leaving. He responded, "You have done well, and I commend you for it. Kindness, even to those in the humblest capacity of life, should be our rule of conduct; and by this act you have won not only my respect but also my esteem."

Why could Fanny be so thoughtful, full of the kindness that causes someone to leave a president to talk to a maid? It's because she understood that her life was not her own. Jesus had captured her heart, and she wanted to live only for Him. She didn't believe someone's value was based on their importance or appearance or wealth. Instead, God had shaped her heart to love all people with His love and to try to be kind to everyone she met.

When she was thirty-eight, Fanny married a fellow member of the Institute for the Blind. Her husband, Alexander, supported her work and used his own musical skills as a gifted organist to write the music for many of her hymns.

One day, a pastor from Scotland told Fanny he thought it was a shame that God, who had given her so many gifts, had not given her the ability to see. She answered him, "Do you know that, if at my birth I had been able to have made one petition to my Creator, it would have been that I should be made blind." The pastor could not understand this and asked her why she said it. "Because," she said, "when I get to heaven, the first face that shall ever gladden my sight will be that of my Savior."

SOURCES

The Sunday-school World, volume 40, issue 8; American Sunday School Union; March 2012.

Fanny J. Crosby, *Fanny J. Crosby: An Autobiography* (Peabody, MA: Hendrickson Publishers, Inc., 2008).

EMPOWERED TO BE KIND

Be kind.

It's easy to say, but hard to do. Sure, it can be easy to be kind to people who are kind to us. But when we think about being kind to a girl who is mean, or to a sibling who pesters, it gets a lot harder. Sometimes being jealous of others leads us to be unkind. Kindness is a struggle for every single person.

For someone who could have lived in bitterness and resentment toward the man whose terrible treatment left her blind, Fanny instead lived a life marked by kindness and joy. This was no accident, and it wasn't because she was simply determined to be a good person. Fanny knew and experienced the kindness of God that led her to trust Him. He helped her not to be angry, but instead to be content with her blindness. Rather than being jealous of those who could see, she lived to show kindness to those who were spiritually blind and needed God to open their eyes to His love and grace.

If we sit around thinking about kindness and trying to "just be kind," we will probably fail a lot. That's because kindness isn't something we can do on our own. We need the love of Jesus and the Holy Spirit inside of us, showing kindness to us and empowering us to show it to others.

You probably won't publish eight thousand songs in your lifetime. You might not know three presidents and multiple members of Congress. You may not live with a difficulty like blindness. But you will have opportunities every single day to choose kindness over bitterness and words of cheer over complaining.

For Fanny, and the rest of us, the secret to being kind comes from the truth in her song,

"Give Me Jesus." When we fill our hearts and minds with the words of Scripture and the beauty of Christ, we won't be as tempted to complain or be bitter. When we know that Jesus is better than anything else, we'll be free to show His kindness to even the most frustrating people in our lives. After all, if He can love us, He can love them too.

QUESTIONS

1. Read Galatians 5:22–23. What does this passage say kindness is?

2. How does fruit grow? Imagine a fruit tree, like an apple or peach tree. Does the fruit make itself grow? Or how does it happen?

3. If you have trusted Jesus Christ and given your life to Him, you have the Holy Spirit living in you. When we spend time with Jesus, the Holy Spirit helps us to know His love for us and to love Him more. And the more we know and love Him, the more like Him we

become and the more fruit we bear. How is this like a fruit tree?

4. Who in your life do you struggle to be kind to? Why?

THEREFORE, AS GOD'S CHOSEN ONES, HOLY AND DEARLY LOVED, PUT ON COMPASSION, KINDNESS, HUMILITY, GENTLENESS, AND PATIENCE.

—COLOSSIANS 3:12

"I ask thee, Oh! Heavenly Father! To make me truly unselfish, to give to me a heart-felt interest in the welfare of others;—a spirit willing to sacrifice my own;—to live 'for the good that I can do!'"

CHARLOTTE FORTEN GRIMKÉ
GODLY AMBITION

Charlotte Louise Bridges Forten was born on August 17, 1837, in Philadelphia, Pennsylvania. As an African American woman growing up before and during the American Civil War, Charlotte was well aware of the terrible treatment of slaves in many American states. She was born into a family of abolitionists—people who spoke, wrote, and argued for the abolition, or end, of slavery.

Charlotte's grandfather, James Forten, served as a powder boy on a ship during the Revolutionary War before traveling to England, where he wouldn't be judged by the color of his skin. During his year there, he met abolitionists like Granville Sharpe, and he came back to America ready to fight against slavery. He'd invented a sailing device that had earned him a great deal of money, but rather than sitting back and enjoying his wealth, he continued to fight for freedom—freedom from slavery, but also freedom for African Americans to be educated and contribute to society.

Charlotte's father, Robert Forten, spoke against slavery and kept Charlotte home for her education, rather than sending her to segregated schools, where black students did not have the same opportunities as white students. He joined the Union Army to fight in the Civil War and died in 1864. He was the first African American to be buried with full military honors.

Her uncle Robert Purvis was an abolitionist whose home was a station for the Underground Railroad. He was known for his efforts to hide hundreds of runaway slaves and to pay for their journeys to freedom. Charlotte's mother and aunts were founding members of a women's anti-slavery society in Philadelphia.

So it comes as no surprise that Charlotte was destined for a life of fighting against slavery and for the equal treatment of all Americans.

When she was sixteen, Charlotte left home for Salem, Massachusetts, where she attended school as the only black student. She loved learning, spending her free time reading the latest poetry and novels and listening to education lectures. At her graduation in 1855, the winning poem from a poetry competition was printed and given to the audience. But no one knew which student had written it. The principal asked the author to step forward in front of a large crowd, and Charlotte walked up. The audience thundered with applause, and Charlotte took another step for the abolitionist cause, proving herself equal to her fellow students and quite talented.

While in Salem, she enjoyed the activities of most teenage girls at the time: studying, practicing music, sewing, and walking by the water and in the hills. She made gingerbread, climbed cherry trees, and visited with friends. And she kept a journal, which was later published as a historical example of what life was like for a young black woman living in the North during slavery.

The day after she began her journal, she wrote about suddenly hearing of a fugitive slave arrested. She wrote that he was:

> Arrested like a criminal in the streets
> of [the] capital, and is now kept strictly
> guarded,—a double police force is
> required, the military are in readi-
> ness; and all this is done to prevent a
> man, whom God has created in his own
> image, from regaining that freedom
> with which, he, in common with every
> other human being, is endowed.

When this slave was sentenced to be returned to slavery, no doubt to be punished severely, Charlotte was distraught. She returned to school determined to work harder so she could "change the condition of my oppressed and suffering people." She longed for her white classmates to understand and feel the sorrow she was feeling. Frequently she found herself in groups where she was the only one who considered ending slavery as supremely important.

Because she saw the cruel treatment of so many of her fellow image bearers, Charlotte had a hard time thinking of her enemies—those who owned slaves—in a Christlike manner. She wrote in her journal when she was sixteen:

> Oh! I long to be good, to be able to meet death calmly and fearlessly, strong in faith and holiness. But this I know can only be through One who died for us, through the pure and perfect love of Him, who was all holiness and love. But how can I hope to be worthy of His love while I still cherish this feeling towards my enemies, this unforgiving spirit? This is a question which I ask myself very often. Other things in comparison with this seem easy to overcome. But hatred of oppression seems to be so blended with hatred of the oppressor I cannot separate them. I feel that no other injury could be so hard to bear, so very hard to forgive, as that inflicted by cruel oppression and prejudice.

There were many people who defended slavery by saying that hard labor was all black people could do—that they were not equal to white people in their mental abilities. Charlotte viewed her efforts in school as an opportunity to prove this argument wrong. She rejoiced whenever she read or heard a fellow African American who showed courage, intellect, and talent. She wrote in her journal about reading the poetry of another woman in this book:

> This evening read 'Poems of Phillis Wheatly,' an African slave, who lived in Boston at the time of the Revolution. She was a wonderfully gifted woman, and many of her poems are very beautiful. Her character and genius afford a striking proof of the falseness of the assertion made by some that hers is an inferior race.

Because she saw injustice so clearly, it was hard for Charlotte to stay quiet in the face of

prejudice. One night at a party when she was surrounded by white attendees, someone said many
people didn't believe George Washington ever
used bad language. Charlotte couldn't help speaking her mind and said she believed that if a person
would own slaves, he might also swear.

After she finished school, she began attending
the Salem Normal School for teachers as its first
African American student. She was thrilled to be
attending and devastated to receive a letter from
her father, instructing her to leave school and
return home to Philadelphia. Teachers assured
her they would do what they could to ensure she
received a teaching job in Salem after graduating
if her father allowed her to stay, and he agreed.
So she remained in Salem, enjoying learning,
but finding it hard to make good friends. Girls
would be friendly to Charlotte in the school-
room, but then if she met them in the street, they
pretended not to know her. She only found one
classmate whom she believed fully supported the

anti-slavery cause and was not prejudiced against people for their skin color.

Charlotte was offered a job teaching in one of Salem's public schools—a first for a black woman in that town. The children were wild and hard to manage, but she stuck with it and prayed for strength to teach them well. Frequently sick, Charlotte had to leave Salem for the warmer weather in Philadelphia. When she left, the Salem newspaper published an article saying they were sorry to hear she was leaving and that she had done an excellent job.

She enjoyed being home with family members, but experienced more racism there than she had in Massachusetts. She was refused entry into two ice cream parlors and a restaurant within a few days, simply because of her skin color. Nicknamed the "City of Brotherly Love," Philadelphia was not the beacon of love and freedom to Charlotte and other black people that it was to many white people. Yet, she was happy to be part of a community of black and white abolitionists who had devoted their lives, energy, and influence to seeing slavery ended.

Every year on the Fourth of July, Charlotte attended a meeting of abolitionists, and she wrote about the hypocrisy of those who celebrated "freedom" with parties while their nation enslaved thousands. This was not freedom for all, just for some.

She longed to do something to help her people and frequently felt helpless and close to despair, writing:

> But oh, how inexpressibly bitter and agonizing it is to feel oneself an outcast from the rest of mankind, as we are in this country! To me it is *dreadful, dreadful*. Were I to indulge in the thought I fear I should become insane. But I do not *despair*. I will not *despair*; though *very* often I can hardly help doing so. God help us! We are indeed a wretched people. Oh, that I could do *much* towards bettering our condition. I will do *all*,

all the *very little* that lies in my power,
while life and strength last!

She fought that despair by reminding herself of what is true—that God is just and would not allow slavery to continue forever.

In her early twenties, Charlotte thought a lot about her life and her legacy—how could she serve others? How could she be less selfish? What good could she do? She prayed, saying, "I ask thee, Oh! Heavenly Father! To make me truly *unselfish*, to give to me a heart-felt interest in the welfare of others;—a spirit willing to sacrifice *my own*;—to live 'for the *good* that I can do!'"

But she struggled with a desire for fame and importance, wanting to do something important for which she could be "forever known." Selfish ambition was a battle, but God would empower her to use her particular gifts and passions in a selfless way in the coming years.

In 1861, the Union military took a strategic hold on the South Carolina coast at Port Royal and the Sea Islands. As a result, most of the white residents of this area fled inland, and thousands of slaves were left behind, freed from slavery but with no jobs or education. The government began sending people to the area who could teach the freed men and women what they needed to know to survive, and they started a school on St. Helena Island in South Carolina.

When she heard about this, Charlotte's friend, the poet John Greenleaf Whittier, encouraged her to apply to go to Port Royal as a teacher. When she was twenty-five, Charlotte sailed from New York to Hilton Head, South Carolina, to be the first black teacher at the Penn School for newly freed children. Arriving on the island, she saw for the first time tall palm trees, live oaks, and hanging Spanish moss. Accustomed to bitterly cold, snowy winters in Salem and Philadelphia, she enjoyed the warm sea breezes of coastal South Carolina, at least until the heat of summer came.

During the day, Charlotte taught the children to read and write at the little brick church building (appropriately named Brick Church), and in the evening, she did the same for the adults on the plantation where she lived. It was a joy to teach so many who were eager to learn. She also became interested in the military troops of black men who enlisted to fight in the Civil War, supporting and nursing them after battles.

On New Year's Day, 1863, President Lincoln's Emancipation Proclamation went into effect, and Charlotte joined in a huge celebration on the island. The people, already free, celebrated the freedom of slaves throughout the country. It was a joy to celebrate with so many who had experienced the horrors of slavery and knew the true joy of freedom. Once such freedwoman was Daphne. Charlotte described her like this:

> . . . she is probably at least a hundred years old. She has had fifty grandchildren, sixty-five greatgrandchildren, and three great, greatgrandchild[ren]. She is entirely blind, but seems quite cheerful and happy. She told us that she was brought from Africa to this country just

after the Revolution. I asked her if she
was glad that all her numerous family
were now and forever free. Her bright
old face grew brighter as she answered,
"Oh yes, yes. . . ."

Charlotte also had the privilege of spending
a day with Harriet Tubman, the heroine of the
Underground Railroad who had risked death
many times to help more than three hundred
slaves escape to freedom in the North. A reward
of $10,000 (which would be close to $300,000 in
today's economy) was offered for her capture by
slaveholders who were angry that she was helping their slaves run away. When Charlotte met
her, Harriet was working in nearby Beaufort,
South Carolina, serving the newly freed men and
women.

Her journal entries during this time in Port
Royal were later published in the well-known
Atlantic Monthly magazine. She described the
joyful "shouts" the people had in the evening—
loudly singing and dancing to songs of praise

they had made up and learned as slaves. The soldiers' courage and bravery, the students' and adults' eagerness to learn—she wrote about it all as a testament to the fact that skin color doesn't determine ability or intelligence. We are truly *all* created equal.

After her time in South Carolina, Charlotte returned to Philadelphia. She eventually met and married Francis Grimké, a pastor whose preaching brought him national attention, due in part to his relentless pursuit of justice and equality for his African American brothers and sisters. She served her husband and their congregation in Washington, DC, and she continued to fight for justice and equality for all people until her death in 1914.

SOURCE

The Journal of Charlotte L. Forten, ed. Ray Allen Billington (New York: W. W. Norton & Co., 1953).

EMPOWERED WITH AMBITION

Ambition is a tricky thing. This "strong desire to do or achieve something, typically requiring determination and hard work" sounds like a great thing. But achieving something just to do it, or to be known as someone important, isn't quite the good thing we might think it is.

Surrounded from birth by people doing important things, giving speeches, writing books and poetry, and working to free slaves, Charlotte probably felt she could never live up to those examples. You might not have the same people around you, but you're probably aware of many famous people—movie stars, authors, musicians. It's easy to get caught up in thinking we should have the same ambition as them—to do something "important."

Charlotte's journal shows her struggle with ambition. She wanted to be known as someone who had done something important, but at the same time she knew that was a *selfish* ambition. Doing something just to be known for it couldn't be right. So what is a *godly* ambition? Is there such a thing?

God gave Charlotte the wisdom through His Word to see that true happiness comes not from thinking of ourselves, but of others. And that's just what happened when she went to South Carolina—she spent her days and nights in serving others, and the temptation for fame and glory was far less important than seeing her fellow image bearers succeed and the glory given to God.

This is the right kind of ambition—the kind that causes us to do our very best so that *God* is given the most glory. It's that kind of determination that frees us from selfishness and helps us to serve others. Charlotte probably never dreamed her journal would one day be published. If she had thought so, she might have written it differently. But God uses what and whom He chooses, and it's our job to be willing and ready for Him to empower and use us, not for our own glory, but for His. And this brings us great joy!

QUESTIONS

---

1. Read Philippians 2:1–4. (Hint: The word *if* in verse 1 is used in this case like the word "since," so Paul is saying something like, "*Since* there is encouragement in Christ. . . .") Look at verse 3 and answer the following:

- We are to do nothing out of:
- Instead, we should:

2. Now look at verse 4. Whom should we care about and look out for? Just ourselves, not ourselves, or ourselves and others?

3. Is it hard for you to care about others? Are some people harder to serve and care about than others? Why?

4. Read on in Philippians 2:5–11. Paul says we should have the same attitude as whom? What kind of attitude did He have?

5. Do you ever feel like Charlotte, wanting to be known for something important?

6. Can you tell the difference between godly ambition and selfish ambition? Think of a time when you had godly ambition and a time when you had selfish ambition. What was the difference between the two?

DO NOTHING OUT OF
SELF AMBITION OR
CONCEIT, BUT IN HUMILITY
CONSIDER OTHERS AS
MORE IMPORTANT THAN
YOURSELVES.
-PHILIPPIANS 2:3

"I thoroughly believe if God gives us a work to do
He will supply physical as well as spiritual strength."

ANNIE ARMSTRONG
WORKING FAITHFULLY

Annie Walker Armstrong was born July 11, 1850, in Baltimore, Maryland. Annie's father died before her second birthday, so she and her four siblings were brought up by their mother, who taught them about her Christian faith and took them to church weekly. They lived in a brick row house in the city without a yard to play in, so they played with neighbors in the streets and sidewalks while families watched from the front steps.

Baltimore was a place of movement. Ships sailed in and out of the harbor, many bringing coffee beans that were roasted upon arrival, filling the air with the scent. Railroads were built, and trains came through, taking passengers throughout the existing American states. People worked hard to provide for their families, and this work ethic was evident in Annie's life as well.

Baltimore was also home to a diverse community of African American, German, and Irish residents. The city saw tension leading up to the

Civil War, and even in Annie's church as a young girl, the congregation was divided between those who supported the North and the South. The war lasted from the time Annie was eleven until she was fifteen. It was not a peaceful time to be growing up. No doubt she heard many frightening, heartbreaking things during this time.

One Sunday during the war, Annie's pastor said these words in his sermon: "The religion of Jesus Christ gives peace in the midst of trouble." Annie wanted the kind of peace she saw in her mother, who had lost a husband and a young son, yet still had hope. She trusted Jesus as her Savior that day.

Annie's mother was interested in foreign missions and helped with a society that raised money to send to missionaries in China, which no doubt inspired Annie's own love for mission work and missionaries. Her friend, Jane Norris, went to China as a missionary when Annie was twenty, making her desire to support missionaries even stronger and more personal.

When she was thirty, Annie heard a presentation about home missions. Previously, she had focused on helping mission work in foreign countries. But as this woman spoke about Native Americans who had been moved from their homes onto reservations, forced to live in poverty, she had a strong desire to help them. A home missions society was formed to raise money to help Native Americans, and they were able to build a school and clothe children in the area that later became the state of Oklahoma.

As the work in foreign and home missions societies grew, Annie realized they needed to start an organization that brought it all together. She was elected the first president of the new Woman's Baptist Home Mission Society of Maryland. Their work included supporting missionaries and efforts in foreign countries, on the American frontier, and in their own city of Baltimore. Annie saw the spiritual and physical needs of people and worked to see that both were cared for.

Eventually, Annie and other Southern Baptist women began the Woman's Missionary Union, although it wasn't easy. Some of the male leaders of the Southern Baptist Convention did not think women should start their own organization. This was over thirty years before the nineteenth amendment was ratified in the US Congress, granting women the right to vote. But Annie felt strongly that Southern Baptist women would best be able to help the mission efforts of their churches through their own organization. She thought woman's work was "a force fore-ordained of God." In other words, she believed this was God's idea and He had equipped women to do this work.

God's strength empowered Annie to see missionaries supported around the United States and the world. She also worked to gain support for two of the first black female Baptist missionaries. Passionate about seeing individual Baptist churches giving to missions, she was constantly writing letters to pastors and leaders, hoping to gain their support. In one year alone, she wrote more than eighteen thousand letters. Working long hours, traveling by train and coach all over America, and serving in Baltimore, Annie was frequently described as indefatigable (someone who "persists tirelessly"). She wrote to a Baptist leader once: "I have no doubt you think I am extremely persistent, but if I get hold of an idea which seems to me to be a good one, I some how do not feel comfortable until I see it carried out, or find that it is out of the question to do anything with it." She suffered physical issues related to her work, but pressed on, relying on the Lord's strength.

It wasn't just supporting other missionaries that kept Annie busy. While she never married or had children, Annie did love and serve children in her church, seeing them as her local mission field. For over fifty years, she taught children from toddlers to age twelve. She would invite the children to her home for afternoon tea, serving them on real cups and saucers and sitting on the floor to play jacks with them. Hearing about a shelter for poor children, she started volunteering and teaching the children there, bringing them hard candy each Sunday afternoon and sharing God's love with them.

Annie wasn't amazing and tireless on her own. No doubt she *was* tired. She worked hard, finding creative ways to teach children about missionaries and to raise missions support. And she worked the whole time without being paid—she refused to accept a salary for her work, saying "it has been a great joy to me that I could feel that while I had not a large amount of money that I could give to the cause of missions, yet I was making an offering of my time."

Some people work hard for money, others for fame. But God gave Annie a heart for Him that desired to reach many people with the good news about Jesus, and she worked in His strength to see that happen. She never wanted recognition or glory, but only "to do the most good and to the greatest number."

Annie's work wasn't without its troubles, though, and she wasn't a perfect leader. No doubt Annie was an intimidating sight to many people at six feet tall, towering over people with her impeccable posture. (Rumor has it Annie's mother had her daughters practice their posture by having them stand against broomsticks.) She naturally experienced conflict with other Woman's Missionary Union workers and with some Southern Baptist leaders. Having strong ideas and opinions about how to do things and what was best, she struggled at times to work with those who disagreed with her. She was sensitive to criticism, but also asked others to help her see if she was wrong about things. Not only did God give her physical and spiritual strength, but she also had to rely on Him for wisdom in difficult relationships.

She also knew God was able to keep her humble. Annie wrote articles about missionaries and other topics of Christian faith for children and adults in Sunday School classes. Sometimes when children wrote to her, she would write them back and include one of her articles. She sent one titled "Our Bible" to a ten-year-old girl named Margaret, hoping she and her friends would help raise money for Bibles. Margaret wrote back, letting Annie know she had found a mistake in the article. Hating to make any mistakes, Annie was sad and embarrassed to find she had, indeed, written a Bible verse reference incorrectly. She remembered Paul's words in 1 Corinthians 10:12: "So, whoever thinks he stands must be careful not to fall." Annie was reminded that it's God's strength and wisdom that we need, not our own.

When she died in December of 1938, at the age of eighty-eight, many people wrote tributes to her, talking about what a great woman she was. Annie probably wouldn't have liked to hear herself praised in that way. Her passion was for the gospel to be preached, not for her own fame or glory. Yet it's clear God did empower Annie to faithfully, relentlessly give her best in everything she did. Her pastor described her as a "dreamer in action . . . one who dreamed her dreams and then made her dreams come true."

Annie didn't see herself as anything special; she just knew God had given her the strength to get things done to the best of her ability. She leaned on Him and dreamed her dreams for His glory.

SOURCES

Bobbie Sorrill, *Annie Armstrong: Dreamer in Action* (Nashville: Broadman Press, 1984).

Keith Harper, ed., *Rescue the Perishing: Selected Correspondence of Annie W. Armstrong* (Macon, GA: Mercer University Press, 2004).

EMPOWERED WITH FAITHFULNESS

In many ways, Annie Armstrong doesn't seem like a typical hero of the faith. She sat in her office and wrote letters or traveled to encourage women in churches around the United States. But that's the point—she was faithful to do what God gave her to do in His strength.

One of the things we learn from Annie is to give our all to whatever God gives us to do. It's easy to see that when we study the lives of women who did things that seem big or important. But for these women, they didn't think they were doing big things. They were just doing the things God put in their hearts to do. They were faithfully serving where God put them.

Ephesians 2:10 says, "For we are his workmanship, created in Christ Jesus for good works, which God prepared ahead of time for us to do." This means that when you trust Jesus for eternal life and saving grace, God has already planned work for you to do for His glory. Do you think a loving God would give you work to do, but then wouldn't give you the power to do it? No way!

In Philippians 2:13, Paul writes that God is the One working in us to do the things He has for us to do: "For it is God who is working in you both to will and to work according to his good purpose."

So what is the work God has for you? Does that only happen later, when you're older? No, He has plans for you right now, right where you are. One of those plans is to faithfully do your best at things like homework and chores. It could mean writing a letter to encourage a friend or baking cookies for a neighbor or babysitting. Maybe you can find a creative way to raise money for a missionary you know. Our lives are made up of ordinary moments and choices, day after day. These are the things He has given you to do.

Whatever He gives us to do, we know God is also faithful to give us the physical and spiritual strength we need, just as He did for Annie.

And like Annie, you may find it hard at times to work with others. Group projects, working with siblings, or deciding whose ideas to implement—these can all be challenges. Sometimes it seems easier just to work alone, rather than having to agree on things with a partner or group. But God is able to give us patience with others and wisdom to work together. Like Annie, at times we will fail at this, but God's grace is abundant, and He will help us.

Ask God what dreams He wants to give you, what work He has for you, and then trust Him to empower you to carry them out in His strength.

QUESTIONS

1. Read Philippians 2:13–16. How does Paul say we should do "everything" in these verses? Why should we do it that way?

2. If God is the one working in us, as Philippians 2:13 says, how does that help us do things without grumbling or complaining?

3. Do you tend to view work as a good thing or a bad thing? Why?

4. How does knowing God gave us work as a blessing change your view of it?

5. What is the work God has given you to do in this stage of life? What are some of your "jobs"?

BE STEADFAST, IMMOVABLE, ALWAYS EXCELLING IN THE LORD'S WORK, BECAUSE YOU KNOW THAT YOUR LABOR IN THE LORD IS NOT IN VAIN. —1 CORINTHIANS 15:58

ESTHER AHN KIM

Born on June 24, 1908; Died in 1997

Graduated from college in Japan, where she became fluent in Japanese

Taught music at a Christian school in Korea

Was the only person out of hundreds who refused to bow to Japanese idols when ordered to do so

Memorized more than one hundred Bible chapters in preparation for her time in prison

Lived in a Japanese prison from 1939 to 1945, depending on God's strength each day

Her book, *If I Perish*, became the all-time religious best seller in Korea and was a best seller in Japan as well.

SOPHIE SCHOLL

Born May 9, 1921; Died February 22, 1943

Was twelve years old when Hitler assumed power over Germany

At age twenty-one, she joined her brother in a secret organization called The White Rose, which wrote and distributed newsletters telling the truth about the injustice of Nazi actions.

Was arrested and accused of high treason after passing out papers at the University of Munich

Before her death, she said she had no regrets and would do it again if she could.

CORRIE TEN BOOM

Born April 15, 1892; Died April 15, 1983

Grew up in Haarlem, Holland (now the Netherlands), as the daughter of a watchmaker

Became the first woman licensed as a watchmaker in Holland

She had a secret hiding place built in her bedroom to hide Jewish people, who were in danger of being arrested and sent to concentration camps. She and her family helped save nearly 800 lives in 3 years.

Arrested and sent to a concentration camp in Germany

After the war, she wrote *The Hiding Place*, which became a best seller, and traveled around the world, telling her story and teaching about God's forgiveness and grace.

BETSIE TEN BOOM

Born August 19, 1885; Died December 16, 1944

Corrie's older sister

Helped with the hiding place and was arrested when she was fifty-eight

In the concentration camp, she encouraged Corrie to practice radical gratitude and thank God for everything, even the fleas that bit them in the night.

She had a vision that after the war, she and Corrie would care for former prisoners and those who had been guards, showing God's love to all of them.

Died in the camp fifteen days before Corrie was released

PANDITA RAMABAI

Born April 23, 1858; Died April 5, 1922

Was one of the first women given the title "Pandita," which means "mistress of learning"

Built a school and house for child widows and orphans and named it "Mukti," which means "salvation" or "freedom"

She faced challenges to her faith and her work from those who didn't like Christianity, but she chose to fear God instead of man.

Rescued more than 2,000 girls and women during 2 famines in India

The organization she started continues today, over one hundred years later.

ELISABETH ELLIOT

Born December 21, 1926; Died June 15, 2015

Studied Greek and translation at Wheaton College in Illinois

Married Jim Elliot in 1953 in Ecuador and had a daughter in 1955

Became a widow when Jim was killed by a tribe in 1956

Later, Elisabeth and her daughter went to live with the tribe who had killed her husband, staying there two years and obeying God's call to preach the gospel to all peoples.

Wrote and published twenty-four books

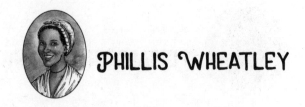

PHILLIS WHEATLEY

Born around 1753; Died December 5, 1784

Captured in Africa and brought to America as a slave when she was seven years old

Named "Phillis" after the ship that brought her to America

Lived in Boston, where a statue of Phillis now stands, during the Revolutionary War.

Was the first African American female poet to have a book published

Used her talent to show the value of all people

JONI EARECKSON TADA

Born October 15, 1949

A diving accident when she was seventeen left her paralyzed and unable to walk or use her hands. God used this to teach her what His abundant life truly means.

Is known for using her mouth to hold a pen, pencil, and paintbrush to create beautiful drawings and paintings

She has written over forty-five books. Her first book, *Joni: An Unforgettable Story*, has been translated into fifty languages.

Her ministry, Joni and Friends, helps people with disabilities and provides wheelchairs to children and adults around the world who can't afford them.

FANNY CROSBY

Born March 24, 1820; Died February 12, 1915

Was left blind after an illness as an infant

Left home at fifteen to study at the New York Institute for the Blind.

Became a well-known hymn writer, penning more than eight thousand hymns in her lifetime

Knew three presidents—John Tyler, James K. Polk, and Grover Cleveland

Believed kindness could accomplish far more than arguments and persuasion

CHARLOTTE FORTEN GRIMKÉ

Born August 17, 1837; Died July 23, 1914

Born into a family of abolitionists in Philadelphia, Pennsylvania

Was the first African American student in two different schools she attended

Was very ambitious but learned the difference between selfish ambition and godly ambition

At twenty-five, she sailed to South Carolina to become the first African American teacher at the Penn School for newly freed slave children.

In South Carolina, she also taught adults who had been slaves and wanted to learn to read and write.

ANNIE ARMSTRONG

Born July 11, 1850; Died December 20, 1938

Started the Southern Baptist Woman's Missionary Union, which helped raise support for missionaries in America and other countries

A tireless worker, she once wrote over 18,000 letters in 1 year.

Refusing to accept payment for her work, she insisted she was giving her time because she wasn't able to give a lot of money.

She was called a "dreamer in action." When she had an idea, she worked faithfully to see it accomplished.

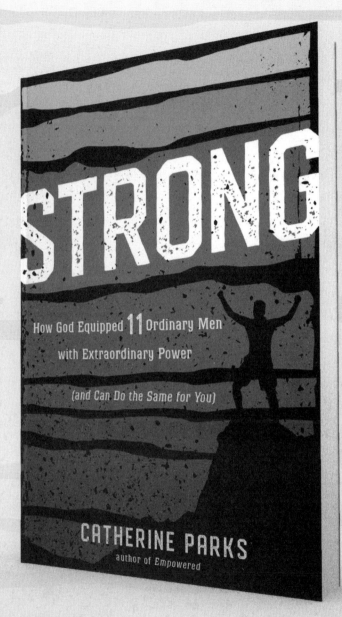

STRONG

How God Equipped **11** Ordinary Men with Extraordinary Power

(and Can Do the Same for You)

CATHERINE PARKS

author of *Empowered*

COMING JUNE 2019!